Thinking Skills Through Science

Sue Duncan
Don McNiven
Chris Savory

Series Editor
David Leat

Chris Kington Publishing

CAMBRIDGE

© Duncan, McNiven & Savory
2004

ISBN 1 899857 55 9

Published 2004 by
Chris Kington Publishing
27 Rathmore Road
Cambridge CB1 7AB
England

British Library cataloguing in publication data.

A catalogue record for this book is available from the British
Library.

Printed in the United Kingdom by:
Halstan & Co Ltd, Amersham, Bucks, England.

Designed by:
Character Design, Hereford, England.

Contents

1 Thinking Skills Through Science 1

2 Developing Thinking in Teaching Science 15

3 The Exemplars   25

4 References   164

Acknowledgements

The authors would like to thank all the science teachers in the following schools for giving of their time to trial many of the activities in this book.

- St. Benedict's High School, Whitehaven.
- Whitehaven School, Whitehaven.
- Western Middle School, Wallsend.
- Settlebeck High School, Sedbergh.
- Throckley Middle School, Newcastle.

After trying out the activities these teachers produced reports of issues arising, strengths and weaknesses and offered many suggestions for the improvement of the content and delivery. Their comments have been carefully analysed and revisions made to the activities as a result. Many of them have been incorporated into the text by providing examples of what to do and what not to do when carrying out the activities. We hope these teachers feel that the activities have been improved as a result.

We are also grateful to other colleagues for useful comments.

S. Duncan
D. McNiven
C. Savory

January 2004

Photocopiable and Electronic Resources

The CD contains copies of all of the pupil sheets, teacher sheets and the spreadsheet files and charts referred to in the exemplars. You may photocopy directly from the book, use the pdf files on the CD to print copies for classroom use, or use the Word files, Excel spreadsheets and charts for producing your own resources or for direct access by pupils on classroom computers. By purchasing the book, you have copyright permission to print and photocopy these within the educational institution in which you work. The Word documents and Excel spreadsheets may be altered to include your own data if you wish. You will find the electronic copy useful to incorporate the suggested alterations, additions and deletions depending on your circumstances and the ability of the pupils. You can make changes as you feel necessary. The electronic material may not be copied or relayed by any means outside the purchasing institution.

Exemplars		
1. Alternative Science Theories	Pupil sheet: Alternative theories	Photocopy or print pdf CDRom Word document
2. A Burning Candle	Pupil sheet: Questions for group discussion	Photocopy or print pdf CDRom Word document
	Pupil sheet: Prompt cards	Photocopy or print pdf CDRom Word document
3. The Carbon Cycle	Pupil sheet: Processes	Photocopy or print pdf CDRom Word document
	Pupil sheet: Constituent parts	Photocopy or print pdf CDRom Word document
4. Climate Change	Pupil sheet: Key scientific points	Photocopy or print pdf CDRom Word document
	Pupil sheet: Widely accepted facts	Photocopy or print pdf CDRom Word document
	Pupil sheet: What is likely to happen?	Photocopy or print pdf CDRom Word document
	Pupil sheet: Uncertainties	Photocopy or print pdf CDRom Word document
5. Diagram from Memory	Pupil sheet: The human digestive system	Photocopy or print pdf CDRom Word document
6. Elements, Compounds and Mixtures	Pupil sheet: Activity 1 - Elements, compounds and mixtures	Photocopy or print pdf CDRom Word document
	Pupil sheet: Activity 2 - Odd one out	Photocopy or print pdf CDRom Word document
7. Energy Transformations	Teacher sheet: Possible starting scenarios	Photocopy or print pdf CDRom Word document
	Teacher sheet: Example system	Photocopy or print pdf CDRom Word document
	Pupil sheet: Energy transformations	Photocopy or print pdf CDRom Word document
	Pupil sheet: Process shapes - cutouts	Photocopy or print pdf CDRom Word document
	Pupil sheet: Energy cards	Photocopy or print pdf CDRom Word document
8. Evaluation of an Experimental Account	Pupil sheet: Version 1	Photocopy or print pdf CDRom Word document
	Pupil sheet: Version 2	Photocopy or print pdf CDRom Word document
	Pupil sheet: Version 3	Photocopy or print pdf CDRom Word document
	Pupil sheet: Evaluation	Photocopy or print pdf CDRom Word document
9. Floating and Sinking	Pupil sheet: True or false?	Photocopy or print pdf CDRom Word document
	Pupil sheet: The sinking of the Titanic	Photocopy or print pdf CDRom Word document
	Pupil sheet: Why do things float?	Photocopy or print pdf CDRom Word document
10. Food Webs	Pupil sheet: Food webs	Photocopy or print pdf CDRom Word document
	Pupil sheet: Predictions	Photocopy or print pdf CDRom Word document
	Pupil sheet: Event or circumstance cards	Photocopy or print pdf CDRom Word document

Photocopiable and Electronic Resources continued

Exemplars		
11. Imagine You are a Sperm Cell	Pupil sheet: Parts of the reproductive system	Photocopy or print pdf CDRom Word document
12. The Solar System	Pupil data sheet 1: Tables 1 and 2 - Planets	Photocopy or print pdf CDRom Excel spreadsheet
	Pupil data sheet 2: Planet mass v gravity	Photocopy or print pdf CDRom Excel spreadsheet and chart
	Pupil data sheet 3: Distance from sun v orbital period	Photocopy or print pdf CDRom Excel spreadsheet and chart
	Pupil data sheet 4: Number of moons v gravity	Photocopy or print pdf CDRom Excel spreadsheet and chart
13. Three Chemical Mysteries	Teacher sheet: Possible outcomes	Photocopy or print pdf CDRom Word document
	Pupil sheet: Mystery 1	Photocopy or print pdf CDRom Word document
	Pupil sheet: Mystery 2	Photocopy or print pdf CDRom Word document
	Pupil sheet: Mystery 3	Photocopy or print pdf CDRom Word document
14. Variation in Humans	Pupil sheets: Charts • Shoe size compared with hand span • Hand span compared with height • Arm span compared with hand span • Shoe size compared with arm span • Circumference of head compared with shoe size • Circumference of head compared with height • Arm span compared with height • Shoe size compared with height • Circumference of head compared with hand span • Circumference of head compared with arm span	Photocopy or print pdf CDRom Excel spreadsheet and charts
	Pupil sheets: Charts with trend lines • Shoe size compared with hand span • Hand span compared with height • Arm span compared with hand span • Shoe size compared with arm span • Circumference of head compared with shoe size • Circumference of head compared with height • Arm span compared with height • Shoe size compared with height • Circumference of head compared with hand span • Circumference of head compared with arm span	Photocopy or print pdf CDRom Excel spreadsheet and charts
	Pupil sheet: Variations data	Photocopy or print pdf CDRom Excel spreadsheet
15. What is Science?	Pupil sheet: Questionnaire	Photocopy or print pdf CDRom Word document
	Pupil sheet: Views about science	Photocopy or print pdf CDRom Word document
	Pupil sheet: Controversial views	Photocopy or print pdf CDRom Word document
16. What Might have Happened?	Teacher information: Racer bicycle and recumbent bicycle	Photocopy or print pdf Web graphs
	Pupil sheet: Racer bicycle and recumbent bicycle	Photocopy or print pdf Web graphs
	Pupil sheet: Parachute	Photocopy or print pdf Web graphs
17. Which Antacid Tablet is the Best?	Pupil sheet: Information about tablets	Photocopy or print pdf CDRom Word document
	Pupil sheet: Analysis of tablets	Photocopy or print pdf CDRom Word document
18. Why Did the Dinosaurs Die Out?	Pupil sheet: Statements	Photocopy or print pdf CDRom Word document

1

Thinking Skills
Through Science

Thinking Skills Through Science

Introduction – what this book is about

This book provides teachers with a series of science activities that will develop pupils' thinking skills. The materials are aimed directly at Key Stage 3 science although it is possible to adapt them for other phases by changing the context for older or younger pupils. The activities described in the exemplars aim to improve and develop pupils' thinking, but the medium for developing thinking skills is a scientific one and development of science knowledge and understanding will occur at the same time.

The thinking skills described and developed in this publication are those identified in the National Curriculum. While exemplars are linked to one specific unit in the *QCA Scheme of Work for Key Stage 3*, other possible links are indicated where appropriate. The exemplars can be incorporated into an individual school's scheme of work.

The materials take account of the principles of the science strand of the Key Stage 3 Strategy. Exemplars are referenced to one of the key scientific ideas identified in the *Framework for Teaching Science: Years 7,8 and 9* (DfES, 2002). These are:

- cells
- interdependence
- energy
- forces
- particles.

The lessons follow the lesson structure recommended by all three Strategies (DfES, 2002) and will be familiar to teachers who have used the best practice of CASE (*Cognitive Acceleration Through Science Education*) for teaching. Teachers need to judge the appropriateness of each exemplar for the pupils and groups that they teach. Thinking skills activities which are easy for some groups will prove challenging for others. Thinking skills teaching and learning (including CASE):

- develops teaching styles which allow pupils to learn more effectively
- encourages pupils to work productively in groups and whole class sessions
- develops pupils' ability to come to grips with cognitive conflicts in evidence and other information, and move on to a deeper or more complex understanding of concepts through a process of construction and metacognition.

Teaching thinking

Carol McGuiness identifies three approaches to teaching thinking (McGuiness, 1999). This book follows the third approach most closely.

1 A generalist approach where a teaching programme is context free, eg Somerset Thinking Skills, or set within a specific curriculum area, eg CASE. This approach assumes that improving thinking in one area can be transferred to others.

2 A subject specific approach – the view that thinking is linked with different disciplines.

3 A combination of these two where a 'thinking curriculum' is developed. In this model, thinking skills and subject specific understanding are taught together.

How to use this book – levels of use

Level 1

Use the exemplars and resources as they are to teach the lesson. Each exemplar is written to a common format:

- Title
- Outline – a brief overview of the exemplar
- Pupils' prior knowledge and skills
- Links to QCA Scheme of Work, thinking skills and key scientific ideas
- Lesson objectives: thinking skills and science
- Context – where the lesson fits in with other content in the curriculum and the context in which it was/can be taught
- Preparation – notes on the classroom organisation and the resources that will need to be prepared

- Introduction – suggested ways of how to carry out the first part of the lesson
- Group work – what you might expect to see if you carry this out with your class
- Plenary – how to manage this part of the lesson and some possible outcomes
- Follow-up – what activities have been carried out following the lesson or some suggestions for what could be done later
- References (where applicable)
- Teacher sheets and pupil sheets in the book and on the CDRom – photocopy pages, print from the CDRom, or use the materials directly on computer.

You can decide whether to use the complete exemplar, or parts of it after reading through the whole. Particular issues to do with the activities described and their management are raised. You will need to be familiar with the background section on lesson structure and teacher behaviours (see pages 6 and 8) to ensure that the exemplar is as successful as can be.

The difficulty of the material varies from exemplar to exemplar. You will be able to assess whether an exemplar is appropriate for a particular group. The exemplars are reports of actual lessons, so necessarily are described and linked to a specific year group. Using the materials with pupils in different years is not difficult (see Level 2 for ideas on adapting the strategies and activities, and also see section on page 8). The most important aspect is linking to pupils' abilities, and your familiarity (hence confidence) with the teaching methodology. Many of the exemplars include some differentiated materials within them.

Links to the National Curriculum can be profitably exploited where a thinking skills lesson is used immediately after relevant background knowledge and understanding has been secured. For example, where pupils have been doing work on the planets, the exemplar on *The Solar System* can be used to focus on relationships using the prior knowledge gained in a previous lesson. Science knowledge and understanding will develop at the same time as thinking skills.

Level 2
Modify the materials for use with other ages of pupils. The same exemplar can be used in different contexts to provide a different level of challenge for older or more able pupils, or with less able groups.

Level 3
By developing pupils' metacognition skills during the plenary session they can improve their understanding of key scientific ideas and epistemology. These skills can be transferred not only to all aspects of science but to other curricular areas too.

Level 4
At a whole school level, teaching thinking is now part of the training provided by the Key Stage 3 Strategy, including both the science and foundation subject strands. Colleagues who have experienced this training can provide useful input into co-ordination at a whole school level. Such co-ordination and a consistent approach across departments will ensure that teachers can deliver a focused 'thinking' strategy across the board.

At the time of writing there is a Thinking Skills Pilot in the KS3 Strategy which includes three departments in a school collaborating in planning and teaching Thinking Skills lessons in order to encourage transfer of learning. This pilot is expected to be available nationally in Autumn 2004.

The exemplars were developed and trialled by different teachers, so there may be some inconsistencies in approach. The 'thinking' notes in the margin are identified by a (T) and a border around them.

Background and Methodology

Links with CASE
CASE has been a pioneering intervention with a proven track record (Adey, Shayer and Yates, 1995). The thinking skills identified in the programmes of study for the *National Curriculum Science Order* (DfEE, 1999) and the *Teachers' Guide to the QCA Scheme of*

Work (QCA, 2000) deal with a broader based thinking strategy for science than the CASE programme. Continuing research has shown that CASE intervention in Years 7 - 9 improves pupils' performance in the end of Key Stage 3 tests and in GCSE, not only in science but also in English and mathematics (Shayer, 1999 and 2000). The CASE materials deal principally with Piagetian reasoning patterns rather than the wider range of thinking skills identified by Carol McGuiness, and now promoted in Key Stage 3 Strategy training. Whilst some of the exemplars described here do generate CASE-style cognitive conflict (because science teachers are already familiar with this method of working), they aim to develop more specific thinking and learning skills in pupils. This book builds on CASE, is a complement to CASE, and takes teaching thinking in science further than before. These materials will provide greater flexibility in both delivering National Curriculum objectives and in developing pupils' capacity as learners.

Teaching thinking can affect pupils' learning in many ways

1 As CASE argues, exposure to cognitive conflict leads to the development of an information-processing capacity, so that pupils engage in more complex thinking. In Piagetian theory this is expressed as being able to use formal operational thinking rather than concrete operations. Such higher-level thinking is fundamental to higher-level achievement in Key Stage 3 and GCSE science. Cognitive conflict is deliberately engineered in many of these activities and exemplars. If pupils are not made to struggle, frown, scratch their heads, complain about being stumped and occasionally admit defeat then they are not doing much worthwhile thinking.

2 Many other thinking skills programmes aim to improve more specific thinking abilities (a good example is Somerset Thinking Skills). The National Curriculum thinking skills programme defines specific skills for pupils in order to aid learning (see below). In addition, some exemplars in this book give explicit attention to visual thinking. By developing a wide range of thinking skills, pupils acquire tools that they can deploy in tackling difficult tasks. The exemplars and teaching activities in this book aim to do just this.

3 Research has suggested that teachers tend to concentrate on teaching subjects in little packets of knowledge and neglect the overarching (or underpinning) knowledge structures that recur and characterise a subject. The overarching concepts are critical in helping pupils see patterns, make connections, understand the subject and apply or transfer their learning. We include in such 'big' concepts, both the schemata that characterise CASE teaching and those in Key Stage 3 science. Teaching thinking allows teachers to bring these concepts and patterns to the fore where they are made explicit and used to develop pupils' understanding.

4 Pupils benefit from metacognition, because without it they cannot effectively use either specific thinking abilities or big concepts. In simple terms metacognition means 'thinking about thinking', but its importance lies in improving pupils' ability to plan, monitor and review their work. Metacognition requires knowledge of thinking (and a language to describe it), skills to monitor and regulate thinking and a disposition to employ the knowledge and skills. Most pupils lack the knowledge, skills and disposition because they have not been given sufficient opportunity to develop them. A good plenary in a good thinking skills lesson provides the perfect stage on which to develop metacognitive awareness.

5 Teaching thinking can improve pupils' self concept, resulting in a positive impact on learning. Many low-achieving pupils have come to believe that they are 'thick' and consequently do not see themselves as successful learners. They withdraw, develop coping strategies or become troublesome. Some high-achieving pupils succeed by producing neat, literate work with little challenge involved. They learn to avoid challenge and shy away from open problems. Many of both groups believe that ability is fixed – you've either got it or you haven't – and they don't invest much effort in learning. Teaching thinking can help pupils change their minds about themselves and about their learning.

6 Teaching thinking means that brainpower is shared. This is developed in Vygotskyan theory. It is important to be clear about the impact on pupils and learning. In

thinking skills lessons pupils work cooperatively and in the process they talk – they interpret, question, clarify and speculate. They are sharing what they know, offering ideas and reasons and receiving feedback. Their thinking is refined and improved. Often the outcome is indeed greater than the sum of the parts. It is through talk that better thinking is developed and in some cases this good thinking is internalised by the individual. Talk is not an optional extra in thinking skills – it is a basic ingredient. Teaching thinking can develop a classroom climate in which pupils can see themselves, to a degree, as a community of learners.

Reflective process and assessment

In using these materials we encourage teachers to reflect on how they are working and the positive effects they are having on pupils. It is through this reflective process that teachers develop their understanding of how to use the exemplars more effectively. If a teacher understands the learning processes in their classroom they have the opportunity to strengthen and refine them.

The teaching of thinking skills helps pupils to learn more effectively. Thus it is important for the teacher and the pupils to be clear about the intended learning outcomes whether they are thinking skills or science outcomes. For this reason possible lesson objectives are listed at the start of individual exemplars. Do not try to cover too many objectives in one lesson. Be selective. One thinking skills objective and one science objective should allow you to assess relatively easily whether or not they have been met. To assist, in each of the exemplars the thinking skills objectives are tracked through the text in the margin notes. Margin notes marked with a (T) inside rules are about 'thinking' objectives. Others are more general to the exemplar.

The references in the QCA *Scheme of Work* to assessment opportunities for checking progress and reviewing work can be used not only to assess pupils' progress in science concepts but also in their thinking skills. It is possible to build time into these activities for pupils to reflect on what they have learnt, how they have learnt, the limitations to their knowledge and what progress has been made in the associated thinking skills.

Thinking skills and the National Curriculum at Key Stage 3

Thinking skills are now embedded in the National Curriculum and a variety of activities within the QCA *Scheme of Work for Key Stage 3* have been identified to enhance these skills. The definitions of thinking skills below are taken from the *Teachers' Guide*.

> 'By using thinking skills pupils can focus on 'knowing how' as well as 'knowing what' – learning how to learn. The following thinking skills complement the key skills and are reflected in activities in all units.
>
> *Information-processing skills*
> These enable pupils to locate and collect relevant information, to sort, classify, sequence, compare and contrast and to analyse part/whole relationships.
>
> *Reasoning skills*
> These enable pupils to give reasons for opinions and actions, to draw inferences and make deductions, to use precise language to explain what they think, and to make judgements and decisions informed by reason or evidence.
>
> *Enquiry skills*
> These enable pupils to ask relevant questions, to pose and define problems, to plan what to do and how to research, to predict outcomes and anticipate consequences, and to test conclusions and improve ideas.
>
> *Creative thinking skills*
> These enable pupils to generate and extend ideas, to suggest hypotheses, to apply imagination, and to look for alternative innovative outcomes.
>
> *Evaluation skills*
> These enable pupils to evaluate information, to judge the value of what they read, hear and do, to develop criteria for judging the value of their own and others' work or ideas, and to have confidence in their judgements.'

Although enquiry skills are not explicitly covered in the exemplars in this book, some elements do occur within the conflict category of science process (see Table 1, page 12). It is assumed that most of these skills will be covered in the teaching of Attainment Target 1 (Scientific Enquiry).

CASE influence on lesson structure

The lesson structure recommended in these exemplars is based on developments from the CASE (North) project. This work, supported by ICI, has further developed CASE processes by emphasising a teaching and learning structure based on four acts within a lesson (Gamble, Savory and McNiven, 2000). In CASE lessons these are:

1 concrete preparation
2 group work involving cognitive conflict
3 a plenary involving construction and metacognition
4 bridging to new and different contexts.

In this book we have further modified this structure to a three-part lesson:

1 introduction
2 group work
3 plenary.

Three part lessons have become accepted as forming the basis for effective lessons, and are becoming widely used (DfES, 2002 and *National Literacy and Numeracy Strategies*).

Starter activities can be included in the introduction to grab pupils' attention and tune them in to the learning that is to follow (see individual exemplars for these suggestions). We have also included suggestions for extension and follow-up work in some exemplars.

Teacher behaviours

To put these exemplars and activities into practice, teachers need to develop their own behaviours (the actions they take, ie what they do) in setting the scene, managing group work and guiding final discussions. The introduction should ensure pupils are clear about the task and will require no further support from the teacher to complete the exemplar. The main part of the lesson focuses on groups of pupils generating cognitive conflict and construction through discussion. In the plenary, the teacher draws out the differences between groups to generate either the 'best' whole group answer (by further construction processes) or pupils' answers that they can support with reasoning, as well as explaining the processes they went through to reach them.

The discussions that take place between pupils during group work are a vital part of the learning process. Research has shown that collaboration, public sharing and revision of ideas are crucial for promoting learning (Peasley, Rosaen and Roth, 1993). In particular, argumentative discussion provides opportunities for pupils to examine their own reasoning and to develop justified explanations that can be articulated to other pupils. It also gives them the opportunity to experience others' views and to evaluate these against their own. In learning to develop and apply the various thinking skills identified in the National Curriculum, group discussion promotes in pupils a deeper understanding of the subject. Meaning and ideas are shared, and pupils begin to use technical language, think and reason in a scientific way.

Many teachers who have tried the method of teaching promoted in these exemplars have been reinvigorated. They have become reflective practitioners and have found that their teaching has improved, and pupils have responded well.

Definition of terms

Objective
What the teacher intends to achieve in terms of pupils' learning.

Outcomes
What pupils (or groups of pupils) have learned at the end of the lesson.

Concrete preparation
The teacher introduces the lesson and sets up the processes for the main activity of the exemplar. Pupils need to be clear about what they are doing and how they will be doing it.

Group work
This is the main pupil activity where cognitive conflict, pupil talk, and construction of new ideas take place. This is thinking.

Class scan
This takes place during the group work. The teacher 'eavesdrops' on the pupils' discussions. The information gained on the thinking processes that are taking place is used to structure the plenary session. This is not an easy thing to do – to stand back without interfering or asking how it's going! It helps to make notes of important points to raise with the whole group later.

Plenary (debriefing)
A whole class feedback/discussion managed by the teacher and sometimes called debriefing.

Transfer
When pupils are able to use the thinking skills they have just been practising in a similar context (eg in the same subject), or in a different context (eg in a different subject), or in everyday life.

Cognitive conflict
Where the pupil finds an idea or observation at variance with their current understanding. It can lead to the construction of new mental models. A similar idea is used in the *Children's Learning in Science Project* (CLIS) where pupils' prior knowledge and understanding are elicited, they are given alternative explanations, and they then reconstruct their understanding.

Metacognition
This is thinking about thinking. Pupils reflect on and articulate the thinking behind their conclusions and how they arrived at these. Such thinking is also used to plan and monitor work.

Teacher behaviours
These are what the teacher needs to do and articulate in each part of the lesson in order to carry out the strategy successfully.

Challenge and support
Teaching thinking makes pupils struggle and think hard. They are generally at the limits of what they can do. Clearly this varies from group to group and individual to individual. Teachers have to work very hard both in planning and teaching to get the level of challenge pitched at a productive level. You want to avoid both a situation in which pupils do not find any aspect of the work an effort, and one in which pupils are lost to the point where they give up. Some general principles and some specific strategies are outlined below, which will aid in getting the pitch right.

1 Some of the best support is provided by pupils themselves, working in groups. At all times encourage them to solve their own problems by thinking it through, as you are trying to reduce their dependence on you and make them more independent. So, for example, if you spot a group who are stuck, get them to tell you what the problem is. This may be enough to get them going. If you need to, tell them to talk it through and you will return in two to three minutes to see if they are still stuck. This principle is strongly related to self-concept as pupils are more inclined to give up when they don't like to take risks.

2 Work with groups that will function. This may mean that you go with friendship groups because they will talk to each other without whining. You may also want to spread your more able pupils or better readers across groups. Over time you can be more adventurous with group composition – non-friendship, mixed gender, mixed learning style preferences. Challenge and learning will be increased by working with a wider range of other minds.

3 Again, over time, you can shift the focus of the learning. In the early stages of working with a class you may decide to concentrate on lessons with obvious science outcomes, so that the onus is on developing understanding of science (eg the *Burning Candle* exemplar). With time you can include activities which bear more on scientific thinking and/or metacognition. This involves giving greater attention to whole class plenaries which explore metacognition (how problems have been solved), and bridge to other contexts in science and more widely.

Adapting the exemplars

Some guidance is given in the individual exemplars on adapting the session for different levels of ability. Some general guidance is given below.

1 Reduce the complexity of information by reducing the number of variables: ie reduce the number of cards, amount of text, or put text on individual cards.

2 Provide supporting information, perhaps through a demonstration, through video or photographs.

3 Ask focused questions that give pupils a handle on where they need to direct their attention.

Lesson Structure

The lessons have been structured in three parts, consistent with the model that has hitherto been successful in CASE science lessons. The outline is given below: Introduction – Group work – Plenary.

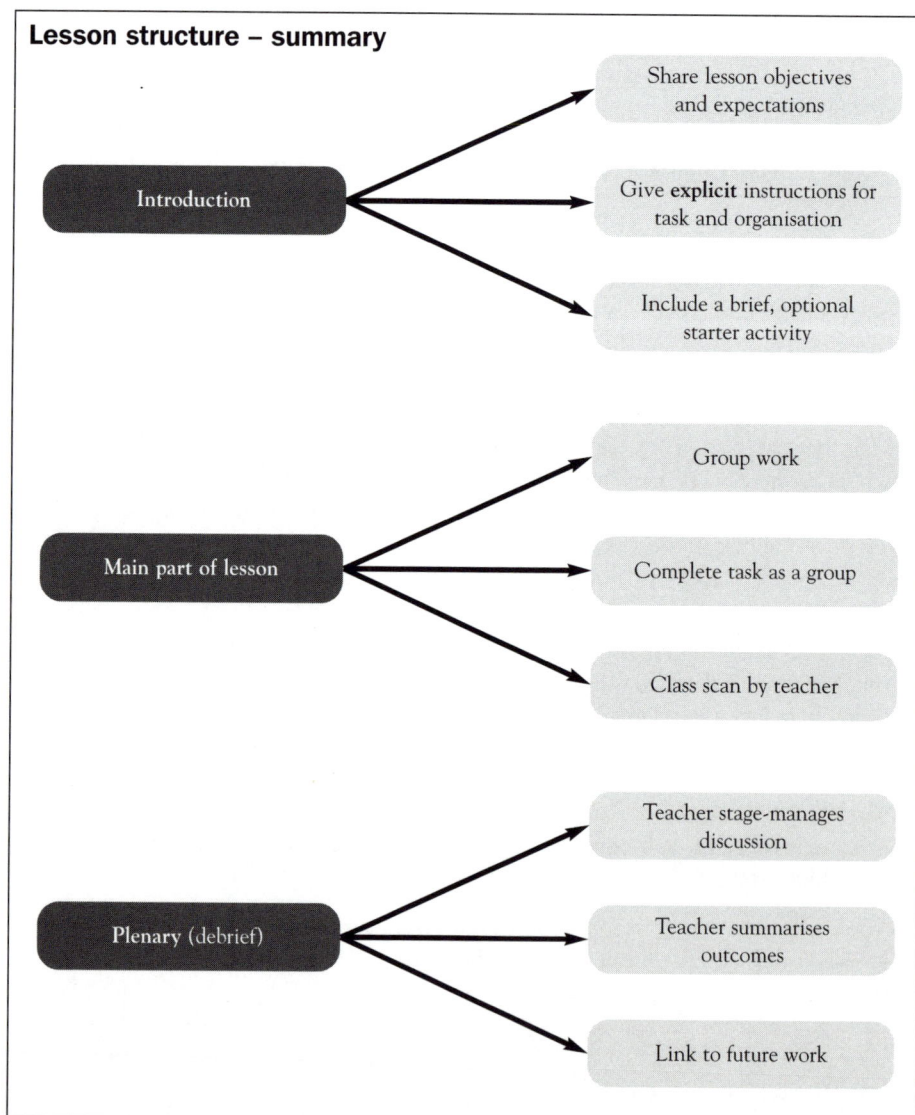

Lesson structure – summary

Introduction → Share lesson objectives and expectations; Give **explicit** instructions for task and organisation; Include a brief, optional starter activity

Main part of lesson → Group work; Complete task as a group; Class scan by teacher

Plenary (debrief) → Teacher stage-manages discussion; Teacher summarises outcomes; Link to future work

Introduction

This sets the scene for the lesson:

1   The objectives (or focus) of the exemplar are clearly explained and shared with the class, emphasising the development of the thinking skills. The teacher needs to have a focused input at this point: pupils need to know the context of the lesson and why they are learning how to think. Include a starter activity at this point if it is appropriate. This should be designed to prepare the pupils mentally for the exemplar, or to elicit prior knowledge or to excite and stimulate them – but it must be brief. For example, it could be a brainstorm, quick revision of the interpretation of different patterns of line graphs, some particularly spectacular visual material, a demonstration, or a story.

2   Make clear your expectations regarding outcomes. Explain what will happen in the plenary. Indicate that feedback on the group outcome will be required and that each group will need to nominate a spokesperson for this purpose. Alternatively, you could nominate a spokesperson for each group which would ensure that over time all pupils have the opportunity to carry out this role and would prevent time being wasted on choosing a 'volunteer'. Establishing the identity of the spokesperson at the outset ensures that pupils can prepare for the feedback. It may be necessary to introduce or reinforce the rules of engagement for group work, especially if there has been little experience of this type of work before.

3   The task should be clearly explained. It is important that pupils know the procedures they need to follow to complete the task successfully. Pupils' talk during the activities should be developing thinking rather than sorting out problems relating to the physical process of carrying out the task. Establish or check beforehand that pupils are confident in any prior knowledge and vocabulary they may need to complete the task.

Group work

Pupils work in groups of three or four to complete the activity. It is important that they recognise the need to come to a group answer which has been agreed via a process of reasoned argument and discussion. Group discussions help construction processes to take place in pupils' thinking. If pupils have not been used to working in collaborative groups to arrive at a group answer, you will need to make clear the ground rules and expectations at the outset.

During this part of the lesson, the role of the teacher is to listen to pupils' discussion. If the introduction has been carried out successfully then the groups should understand the task and will therefore not need to ask for further clarification. In the event of pupils needing reassurance or not having much confidence in their own abilities, the teacher should encourage them to solve their own problems. Prompts such as 'try to agree among yourselves what to do and I'll come back and check in a couple of minutes' might be helpful.

You should note, mentally or on paper, outcomes and arguments in each group. This 'class scan' will be used to manage the plenary. This is perhaps one of the most challenging parts of the lesson for a teacher to carry out. It is difficult not to interfere with the group, even just to ask how they are getting on. Just listen in to the discussion. It is vitally important that pupils are allowed to carry out their own discussions without teacher input.

Plenary (Debriefing)

This is the most important part of the lesson. Plenty of time must be built in for it. Stage-manage this part of the lesson in the light of outcomes from the group work by ensuring that all groups are required to contribute. From the information gathered during the observation of the group discussions, you will know what each group has produced and the processes they went through to arrive at their answer. The idea is to encourage pupils to explain their thinking and if possible to encourage the construction of ideas at a whole class level. Your questioning skills are important here. To encourage pupils to explain their thought processes and the stages of their discussion which led them to arrive at their conclusion, use open questions and phrases such as:

'Can you explain why your group thought…'
'Go on…'
'Say a bit more'
'Why?'
'I heard your group say something interesting. Can you explain it to the rest of us?'
etc…

You need to manage the class discussion so that all pupils feel that their contribution is valued. Manage contributions to preserve a logical sequence. This may be difficult as pupils' ideas will/may change as the discussion progresses. Don't start, therefore, with the 'best' group, and don't allow a group to be ridiculed because of lack of progress or a 'wrong' answer. Allow less able groups to make a contribution too.

Finally, round off the lesson by summarising the thinking processes which have been used, as well as the science outcomes. Discussion in a plenary can usefully highlight misconceptions that pupils may hold. If this occurs you will need to plan future lessons to explore these further and to correct them. The plenary is important to allow pupils to become better thinkers and learners. They do this if they are given the opportunity to think about and understand more about the process of thinking (metacognition). They may not be familiar with giving extended answers or explanations. So, make sure they are given time to think before they have to answer. You could use strategies such as counting slowly to thirty (silently!) before expecting an answer. If this silence proves too threatening, allowing a period of discussion with other pupils and then accept a group answer.

Materials
The worksheets that pupils will need for the activities are provided as photocopiable masters at the end of each exemplar. They are also on the CDRom together with the Excel spreadsheets and charts you will need for the *Variation* and *The Solar System* exemplars.

Links
Table 1 lists the exemplars, and identifies the links between key scientific ideas, cognitive conflict and thinking skills. (see page 12)

Table 2 shows how the exemplars link to key scientific ideas, year groups and *QCA Schemes of Work*. (see page 13)

Bridging
Bridging activities require pupils to use the thinking skills they have practised in one lesson in a different context. The application of thinking skills can be in science or in a different subject. Bridging activities help to embed learning. They enable pupils to see links, not only between subjects they learn in school but also between these and their everyday lives. Just like plenary sessions, bridging activities need to be planned. You will need to decide which particular thinking skill to focus on, and what type of bridging activity to use. Some are described in the following paragraph:

Quick method. The temptation is to use the simplest and quickest method, ie to tell the pupils an example and perhaps include a brief demonstration of some sort.

Follow-up lesson. If your science lessons are short and you are pushed to plan for a plenary let alone a bridging session, you might like to consider having a follow-up lesson where the thinking skill is applied in a new context. This may be in a science context, or if you have enough time, you could spend another lesson looking at the skill in a non-science context.

As a starter. During a starter activity pupils can be reminded of the thinking they were developing in a previous lesson. For example, if visual memory is being developed, refer to the *Drawing from Memory* exemplar they did. Their diagrams could be used as a stimulus.

Other subjects. If teaching thinking is well established in your school, talk to your colleagues. It is quite possible that the geography teacher could, for example, include reference to the thinking which pupils have developed or practised in science in a relevant geography lesson.

Recall. In some lessons, you may be able to ask pupils to identify thinking skills they have used previously and the context in which they were used. Possibilities could include CAME (*Cognitive Acceleration Through Maths Education*) and Somerset Thinking Skills. This will encourage pupils to make their own bridges in their learning.

Whichever method you use, remember that pupils need to be able to transfer skills and to see links. You need to plan to teach this.

Developing activities of your own

Teaching thinking skills is more than just a 'bolt-on' activity. It forms an integral part of teaching the curriculum, whether science or other subjects. Many CASE practitioners cover some aspects of Sc1, but do not always directly relate them to the National Curriculum in science. Unfortunately, bridging activities, which could do this, are all too often omitted because of lack of time.

But, it is the process which is important. By using and extending the processes developed in this book, further and more efficient learning can be achieved. The thinking skills developed here can be extended by further activities which you have developed yourself, and which expand your pupils' thinking skills to develop understanding of scientific concepts in the National Curriculum. These processes become part of your everyday teaching of science and are therefore used to develop scientific understanding as well as thinking skills.

In developing further materials, remember that it is more productive for the department to work together on this rather than individuals producing their own materials. Manage the development and incorporate the new activities into a departmental scheme. Assessment may also be an issue that you may wish to consider as a whole department.

A relatively straightforward method initially is to adapt one of the exemplars in this book to another context. There are already some examples. See for instance, creativity – in imagining you are a carbon atom in one exemplar or a sperm in another (see pages 38 - 43 and 98 - 101). *The Diagram From Memory* can be used for other organ systems or for relatively complex electrical circuits (see pages 56 - 59). The same exemplars can also be used in Key Stage 4 or in even more advanced science contexts.

You may find that some adaptations will not develop the necessary conflicts in order to deepen understanding. In which case, try another thinking strategy, or adapt another exemplar. Suggestions for extension and adaptation have been made at the end of some of the exemplars. It is up to you to develop them to suit your teaching style, and your pupils' needs.

To develop further activities:
- consider whether the topic includes the development of a concept
- decide on the lesson objectives – science and/or thinking skills
- consider if and where opposing or conflicting evidence or information has hitherto hindered the understanding of the concept
- develop appropriate activities, investigations, materials, worksheets and/or questions that will expose these conflicts and allow pupils to wrestle with the evidence
- use the same lesson format, ie break up the lesson into introduction, group session and plenary
- trial the lesson and refine it.

Table 1: Summary of Exemplars

Exemplar	Key scientific idea	Cognitive conflict	Thinking skills
1. Alternative Science Theories	Interdependence	Understanding argument	Reasoning Creative thinking
2. A Burning Candle	Particles	Science process	Reasoning Enquiry
3. The Carbon Cycle	Interdependence	Visual thinking	Reasoning Creative thinking Information processing
4. Climate Change	Interdependence	Understanding argument	Reasoning Evaluation
5. Diagram from Memory	Cells	Visual memory Metacognition	Information processing Creative thinking
6. Elements, Compounds and Mixtures	Particles	Science process	Information processing Evaluation
7. Energy Transformations	Energy	Visual thinking	Creative thinking
8. Evaluation of an Experimental Account	Interdependence	Science process	Evaluation
9. Floating and Sinking	Forces	Science process Understanding argument	Evaluation
10. Food Webs	Interdependence	Science process Metacognition	Reasoning
11. Imagine You Are a Sperm Cell	Cells	Visual thinking Metacognition	Sequencing Creative thinking
12. The Solar System	Forces	Science process	Information processing Reasoning
13. Three Chemical Mysteries	Particles	Science process Metacognition	Information processing Evaluation
14. Variation in Humans	Interdependence	Visual thinking	Information processing Evaluation
15. What is Science?	All key ideas	Understanding argument	Reasoning Evaluation
16. What Might Have Happened?	Forces	Visual thinking Science process	Information processing Reasoning Evaluation
17. Which Antacid Tablet is the Best?	Particles	Science process Metacognition	Evaluation
18. Why Did the Dinosaurs Die Out?	Interdependence	Science process Understanding argument	Creative thinking Hypothesising

In this publication, science process is defined as a combination of procedural understanding and the application and development of science knowledge and understanding. *The National Curriculum Science Orders* identify four areas for study in investigative skills:

- planning
- obtaining and presenting evidence
- considering evidence
- evaluating.

Table 2: Summary of Exemplars

Exemplar	Aimed at Year	QCA main link unit	Other QCA unit links	Key scientific idea	Thinking skills
1. Alternative Science Theories	8	8C	7F, 7L 8E, 8K 9A, 9H	Interdependence	Reasoning Creative thinking
2. A Burning Candle	7	7F	8E, 8F	Particles	Reasoning Enquiry
3. The Carbon Cycle	9	N/a	7F, 7I, 7L 8A, 8B, 8G 9B, 9D, 9E, 9G, 9H	Interdependence	Reasoning Creative thinking Information processing
4. Climate Change	9	9G		Interdependence	Reasoning Evaluation
5. Diagram from Memory	8	8A		Cells	Information processing Creative thinking
6. Elements, Compounds and Mixtures	8	8E	8F	Particles	Information processing Evaluation
7. Energy Transformations	9	9I		Energy	Creative thinking
8. Evaluation of an Experimental Account	8	8I	8D	Interdependence	Evaluation
9. Floating and Sinking	7	7K		Forces	Evaluation
10. Food Webs	7	7C		Interdependence	Reasoning
11. Imagine You Are a Sperm Cell	7	7B		Cells	Sequencing Creative thinking
12. The Solar System	7	7L		Forces	Information processing Reasoning
13. Three Chemical Mysteries	7	7H	8F	Particles	Information processing Evaluation
14. Variation in Humans	7	7D		Interdependence	Information processing Evaluation
15. What is Science?	7	N/a		All key ideas	Reasoning Evaluation
16. What Might Have Happened?	9	9K	9J	Forces	Information processing Reasoning Evaluation
17. Which Antacid Tablet is the Best?	7	7F	8H, 9E (extension)	Particles	Evaluation
18. Why Did the Dinosaurs Die Out?	7	7C		Interdependence	Creative thinking Hypothesising

Thinking Skills Through Science

2

Developing Thinking in Teaching Science

Developing Thinking in Teaching Science

Professional Development

As a result of reading this book and trying out some of the exemplars and activities you may find that you need to change your teaching. This can be a challenge, and will certainly be easier and more successful if you have some support. The ultimate goal of course is to improve pupils' learning by developing their ability to think. Teaching thinking is different – and practice makes perfect. It is tempting to abandon a new strategy if it doesn't go as well as you hoped the first time. So what affects your teaching and your pupils' learning and how can professional development help? Pupils respond to what a teacher does or does not do and their learning is either improved or impeded. Teacher development aids pupil development. What teachers do, ie how they behave, depends on their knowledge and their beliefs. A teacher's subject knowledge and their knowledge and understanding of different teaching techniques will affect the accuracy of their instruction and the confidence and skill with which they impart information to pupils.

A teacher's knowledge will also include their knowledge of the pupils they are teaching. This is more than knowing their names: a teacher needs to have an accurate assessment as to where pupils are and what they need to do next to improve. Expectations need to be realistic but high. Knowing how pupils prefer to learn will also help when planning a teaching strategy. The feedback from pupils in terms of their responses will enable the teacher to refine and improve new strategies. If pupils indicate that they enjoyed the lesson, felt that they had made good progress in their learning and if they behaved well, the teacher will feel the lesson was a success and use the same techniques again. If, on the other hand pupils do not respond well, become bored and misbehave or if the teacher feels that new strategies have not enabled pupils to learn as much, then professional support will enable the teacher to assess the reasons why – and improve their teaching – rather than abandon the new technique at the first hurdle.

Teacher's beliefs, for example in the 'basic truths' of what makes a good scientist, why and how pupils should be taught science, will affect how readily and therefore how effectively they embrace new ideas. For teachers used to 'concrete' outcomes, 'thinking' lessons such as those in this book will present a challenge. Changing teachers' beliefs is usually harder than changing their knowledge.

All these aspects of a teacher's work can be improved by professional development, as shown in the Figure.

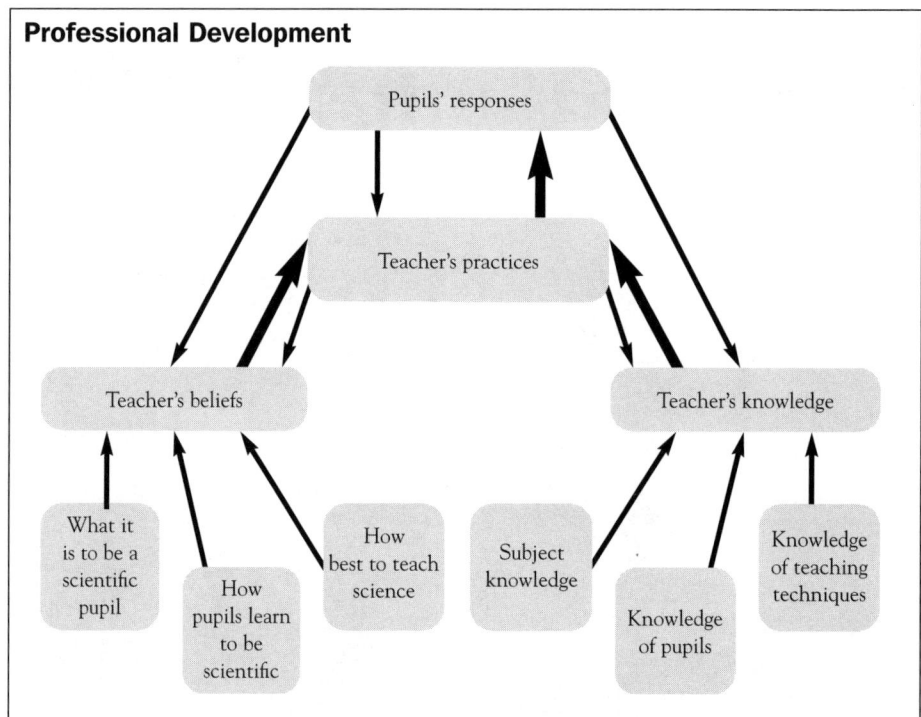

Professional Development

Adapted from Askew et al (1997) *Effective Teachers of Numeracy*

No matter how carefully you read the introduction to this book and no matter how thoroughly you plan, carry out and evaluate the lesson, nothing can beat support from colleagues and / or professional training to help you perfect your techniques. Some ways you can do this are:

1 Develop 'teaching thinking' as part of the Key Stage 3 Strategy. You may find that other departments in the school are developing thinking skills lessons. Join with them to work across different departments. Consultants may be available to work with you – not only science consultants but also those working in the foundation subjects. Check with the head of department or school strategy manager, and get involved with whole school developments.

2 Work with colleagues in your department. Plan lessons together, team-teach, or watch each other teach.

3 Get yourself videoed and watch the video of your lesson – alone in the first instance if needs be – but preferably with a supportive colleague who is familiar with some of these techniques. This will enable you, in relative comfort, to reflect on your successes and identify where the lesson could be improved. Look for the positives. An advantage of watching a video of yourself teaching is that it allows you to do this. It's all too easy when you reflect on a lesson, (particularly one where you've tried a new strategy) to dwell on what went wrong. If you do this you'll give up and never move forward. You'll probably need to watch the video through several times. The first time allows you to get over the initial shock of seeing yourself teaching. Subsequent viewings allow you to concentrate on what you were doing (your teacher behaviours) and what learning resulted from this.

4 Participate in Teaching Thinking and CASE training. This will provide the theoretical background and explain the principles behind these methods of teaching. The skills you develop are transferable and can be used effectively in all lessons.

5 Contact your local science adviser for details of trainers – who they are and how you can access their help. From 2004 all LEAs will have access to training modules in coaching as part of the KS3 Strategy.

Experience has shown that working with other teachers or consultants will help you to develop new teaching strategies more effectively than working alone. Parallel experiences can be found in the development of skills in other areas of life such as sports, crafts etc. You progress much faster with a supportive coach than if you try to improve alone. That way there is no danger of reinforcing, or not identifying, poor practice.

Learning and Teaching: A Strategy for Professional Development (DfEE, 0071/2001) clearly shows that coaching provides a structure through which to implement most of the activities that are reported to impact on classroom practice:

1. Opportunities to learn from and with other teachers, in their own or other schools:

- by observing colleagues teaching and discussing what they have observed
- through collaborative enquiry into real school improvement problems, drawing on best practice in developing solutions
- by taking part in coaching or mentoring.

2. High quality focused training on specific skill areas, underpinned by excellent teaching materials and direct support to apply their learning back in the classroom.

Furthermore, research shows that successful professional development is characterised by the chance to:

- experiment with new ideas
- understand the rationale behind those ideas
- have explicit coaching and feedback
- have support by head teachers
- participate in wider teacher networks.

Classroom observation

Developing your skills in teaching thinking will probably involve lesson observation. Your school may already have systems and protocols in place for classroom observation either as part of performance management procedures or as part of the school self-evaluation. LEA consultants will also have observed many teachers as part of the Key Stage 3 Strategy. If you are going to practise observing lessons as part of the development of teaching thinking strategies, it is important that you consider the following:

1 The purpose and focus of the observation should be agreed between the observer and the observed.

2 Observe / be observed by a colleague you feel comfortable with, and whom you respect. If you are working with a colleague who is acting as your coach, you need to be confident that they know more than you do and can give you constructive feedback to help you improve.

3 Make sure there are no obstacles to the observations. Your time should be protected. The school should provide cover and your observer should not have to leave your lesson.

4 Build in time for reflection and a feedback discussion. Don't try to do this in the prep room at lunchtime but build in adequate 'quality' time.

5 Clarify ground rules, eg who is in charge of discipline, what level of participation is expected of the observer etc.

Positive outcomes from structured, supportive classroom observation include:

- more reflective practitioners
- a greater variety of teaching and learning strategies
- more sharing of good practice between departments
- development of a whole school focus.

Curriculum Planning

Changes to a department's curriculum can take place as a result of a number of different stimuli and at different levels. A head of department could be required to incorporate changes as a whole school initiative or as a result of a departmental decision. In either case, the relevant information, timescales, resources, training, monitoring and evaluation of impact etc will need to be incorporated in the departmental planning documentation. The head of department will need to be skilled in the management of change. On the other hand, a teacher could decide to effect a change to his or her own lessons, perhaps as a result of a professional development experience. The planning for introducing the change would then only need to appear in the short (or perhaps) medium term plans in the first instance.

By including thinking skills activities in your scheme of work you will be increasing the range of opportunities pupils have to learn in a variety of ways. In many science lessons pupils have traditionally focused on the logical and mathematical aspects of learning. The exemplars in this book provide opportunities for pupils to experience a wider range of learning styles. All activities, for example, involve discussion in groups which enables those pupils who prefer verbal communication to practise their preferred learning style and those who need encouragement to develop their oral skills to do so in a supportive group. By careful planning, a range of such thinking skills can be developed at regular intervals throughout the academic year. Such work can make a major contribution to literacy across the curriculum, which stresses the importance of both speaking and listening.

1. Long term planning
Incorporating thinking skills

The focus of these materials and exemplars is on developing pupils' thinking and analytical skills as described in the thinking skills element of the *Lesson objectives*. Improving pupils' skills in these areas makes for better progress through the content of the Key Stage 3 curriculum. Pupils are able to see links and make connections within the wider programme of study. If you are using the QCA Scheme of Work you will be able to see directly where each exemplar fits (as described in the *Links* section at the start of each exemplar). In some cases the materials provide an alternative activity, eg *Burning Candle* can be used in part 4 of QCA Unit 7f. If you are not using the QCA Scheme of Work, you will be able to slot the exemplars into your planning relatively easily. After all, the programme of study that you are following is the same. You need to identify where these activities best fit in to your own scheme of work.

Although the materials in this book are linked to the QCA Scheme of Work, the activities can be carried out in line with the relevant science context. Or you can sequence the activities to take account of the programme of thinking skills you have devised as well as the science objectives.

Scientific enquiry
The need for pupils to evaluate is part of the programme of study for scientific enquiry (Sc1). In the *Framework for Teaching Science: Years 7, 8 and 9* the yearly teaching objectives are as follows:

> **'By the end of Year 7** *it is expected that pupils should be able to evaluate the strength of evidence.*
>
> **By the end of Year 8** *pupils should be able to consider whether an enquiry could have been improved to yield stronger evidence.*
>
> **By the end of Year 9** *they should be able to describe how evidence supports a conclusion and to identify the limitations of evidence.'*

> (DfES, 2002)

Teaching enquiry skills explicitly will help them achieve these yearly teaching objectives. Your planning should include objectives for Sc1. Slotting in an exemplar that links with one of these objectives could be more appropriate than linking it with the knowledge and understanding aspects of the curriculum.

Oral and discussion skills
These exemplars and activities depend for their success on pupils being able to express themselves clearly and articulate their arguments. If your pupils are not used to participating in discussions, challenging others' thinking, and explaining the reasoning behind their own arguments they will need to be introduced to these techniques and the language and behaviours that are necessary for success.

Vocabulary
Check with other departments that you use common vocabulary when teaching thinking. You could also try to ensure in your long term planning that the agreed terminology is introduced at the same time.

2. Short/medium term planning
Use the exemplars and activities to plan your lessons in the usual way. Don't forget that the plenary is a critical part of a thinking skills lesson. It is crucial that this time is planned carefully. Your short term planning should take account not only of the time you will need but also (until you become more expert) the way that this part of the lesson will be managed. After the lesson reflect on the successes and what you need to do to improve the learning the next time you teach in this way. Make notes on your plan so that you will be able to incorporate any necessary changes in future lessons.

3. The following checklist provides a summary for curriculum planning:
- check with your head of department/school strategy manager what the school's position is regarding teaching thinking
- select an exemplar that fits in with your current scheme of work, a suitable topic or unit or appropriate Sc1 objectives
- plan and teach the lesson
- evaluate and modify it in the light of experience
- try other exemplars in order to increase the development of pupils' thinking

- incorporate exemplars into the scheme of work for science
- write new exemplars using the principles for teaching thinking outlined in this book (see *Developing activities of your own* on page 11).
- make links with other teachers in your school, working together through other subjects to develop whole school teaching thinking strategies.

Bridging

Some key points about bridging were made in *Section 1* (see pages 10 and 11). This chapter contains examples of bridging activities that could be used with some of the exemplars. Suggestions are given below under the headings of **conflict category**, as referred to in Table 1 (see page 12), and **specific exemplars**. These opportunities for bridging are by no means exhaustive, but are discussed briefly to indicate the range of possibilities.

Examples based on conflict category

Understanding argument

Climate Change focuses principally on argument and deals with conflicting evidence which leads to no single correct answer. It offers a number of bridging opportunities to other curriculum areas. For example, in history similar reasoning can be used to analyse the reasons for an historical event, its consequences, different interpretations of its significance and links with other events and changes. In geography there is a direct link to climate variation as well as the opportunity to extend the reasoning process to explore environmental management.

In everyday life such reasoning skills find ready application in activities such as deciding which sorts of food to buy – organically-grown produce, high fibre, reduced sugar varieties etc.

Other exemplars which lend themselves to make bridging links in developing and understanding argument include *Alternative Science Theories*, *Why Did the Dinosaurs Die Out?*, *Floating and Sinking* and *What is Science?*

Science process

The Solar System involves the extraction and ordering of evidence to look for relationships. This type of activity has wide applications across the curriculum (eg handling data in mathematics, resource depletion in science and geography) as well as to everyday life (eg braking distances for vehicles or extraction of relevant data from a train timetable).

Other exemplars that could be used to make similar bridging links include *Variation in Humans* and *Elements, Compounds and Mixtures*.

Visual thinking

The Carbon Cycle can readily provide a bridge to other cycles within science, eg nitrogen or water cycles. More widely it can be linked to revision activities involving cycles or flow charts that connect curriculum content and processes together. Similar reasoning and information-processing skills can be used for systems and control in design and technology, and patterns and processes in geography, including the rock cycle.

Other exemplars that can bridge in a similar way include *Food Webs* and *Diagram from Memory*.

Examples based on specific exemplars

Diagram from Memory

To carry out this exemplar pupils identify the component parts of the structure, remember them and reconstruct the diagram. They also work out within their small group the strategies they will need to carry out this task. In reconstructing the diagram they develop their understanding of the processes of digestion as they relate the structure of the alimentary canal to its function. The same process can be used with other organ systems, eg redrawing a stylised diagram of the heart will use group thinking processes to understand the circulation through the heart. The diagrams could then be used to assess pupils' understanding of the circulatory system. This bridging activity could be done to consolidate knowledge and understanding towards the end of a session on the heart structure.

Another possibility may be to use diagrams that involve the use of symbols such as electric circuits. A complex circuit diagram that pupils are unfamiliar with such as one involving a relay or several interlinked circuits could be used. Pupils would have to think about and understand the function of electric circuits in order to complete the diagram.

The use of symbols on maps is an obvious bridge to geography. Pupils could be asked to memorise the route from A to B and redraw it including all the relevant symbols and landmarks. This task develops pupils' geographical understanding and visual memory, and also tests their thinking and interpretation. Successful completion of this task requires more than knowledge of map symbols. Bridging into everyday life is evidenced by a need to use and understand maps during travel or interpret diagrams in instruction books.

Elements, Compounds and Mixtures
This exemplar concerns the selection of criteria for grouping things together. The process of selecting an odd one out is one which we all do every day, for example, when choosing which clothes to wear. The skills of selection and an ability to understand the reasons for doing so are developed. These skills can be bridged to many contexts both in science and in other subjects.

In science, the structure of the periodic table is the result of a grouping process involving, at a simple level, the chemical properties of elements. Likewise, classification of plants and animals presents a similar process, as does any selection of substances/materials by physical properties for a particular purpose, eg electrical or thermal conductivity, density in floating and sinking etc.

Energy Transformations
This exemplar is about the use of a given set of rules (in this case, allowable energy forms and acceptable transformations) to get from point A to point B. It is about using creative thinking to solve problems within given constraints (the rules), using as many steps as possible. More commonly, however, the process involves finding the shortest path. The process is the same.

These techniques can be bridged to mathematics (solving equations, trigonometric identities) or English (anagrams). In forensic science, analysis of unknown substances involves a similar process. The balancing of a beam on a fulcrum by using the principle of moments involves a similar selection of mass and distance, with the added possibility of pushing from below the beam.

Floating and Sinking
There are two thinking techniques used in this exemplar. The first – 'true or false' – allows pupils to weigh up contributing information in order to come to a decision. The decision is made easier if there is also a possibility of a partially true outcome. One can think of other contexts where this is applicable within science – element/compound, metal/non-metal, conductor/insulator, plant/animal. This process can be extended to identify the contributory factors to an overall principle – as indeed in the topic of this activity: floating and sinking. This allows the building up of the concept by the sum of its contributory factors. Other concepts, which could be investigated by a similar thinking strategy include plant growth, factors which influence current in an electrical circuit, how we see coloured objects, the difference between weight and mass, pressure, factors involved in population growth and decline, contributory factors in the propagation of disease, etc.

The second technique involves assessing the importance of the contributory factors by a process of discussion and construction. This process involves the teacher in identifying not only these factors, but also plausible distractors / red herrings to enable cognitive conflict to arise. This technique can be used to extend other exemplars in this book, such as *Why Did the Dinosaurs Die Out?* and *What is Science?* Other contexts could include investigation of volcanoes and earthquakes, photosynthesis, adaptation to habitat, how life evolved from chemicals, global warming and many other controversial issues.

Three Chemical Mysteries

'Mysteries', as a tool for developing thinking, are described in the sister publication *Thinking Through Geography* (Leat, 2001). David Leat describes a *Mystery* as '*probably the most powerful strategy*' for developing thinking skills, because it can completely transform the teaching and learning process. However, the *Mysteries* described in this book are not so open-ended as those in geography, since there is probably an answer which, it could be argued, is the correct one. Nevertheless, the process is the same, involving argument and discussion through construction and metacognitive processes.

As well as the forensic case described, *Mysteries* in science could involve identification of plants and/or animals from information such as identifying features, where they grow/live and feeding habits.

Which Antacid Tablet is the Best?

This exemplar develops the concept 'best'. Best is subjective, meaning different things to different people. Identification of the factors involved may not be subjective, but deciding on their priority certainly is. Group agreement develops skills of analysis, negotiation and tolerance through a process of collaborative discussion. Pupils are constantly meeting this type of thinking in their everyday lives – the best CD, best singer, best burger, etc!

Science presents other contexts which can develop these skills such as best Christmas tree lights, or best material for absorption or reflection of heat in given circumstances. It is the circumstances that usually develop the conflict as the scientific facts are usually fixed. You can no doubt think of many other examples.

What Might Have Happened?

This exemplar involves a process that uses prior knowledge and an understanding of the behaviour of the process, to identify 'what might have happened, if...' More than one interacting variable creates the possibility of cognitive conflict. So, in this case, information / knowledge is gained in the form of a velocity/time graph. The time factor is important in enabling a discussion of what has occurred. However, outcomes could also enable a decision on past events to be evaluated. Thus a charred mass shows evidence of a fire, tide marks of a flood, and so on. This sort of evidence, however, leads one into the *Mysteries* scenario described under *Three Chemical Mysteries*. For example, there could be evidence of failure of electricity supply, melting ice, etc. which could lead to an identification of what might have happened. Bridging more closely to the type of scenario described in this exemplar can be seen from:

- graph plots of temperature changes (as in a cooling curve involving changes of state)
- amount of electricity used over time (identifying appliances which were used at a particular time)
- mass/volume of carbon dioxide released over time from a carbonate/acid reaction (identifying particle size/concentration, etc).

Cognitive Conflict

Table 1 in *Section 1* identifies some of the areas of conflict pupils will encounter in each exemplar (see page 12). The classification is not intended to form a definitive list but is presented as a tool for planning. By identifying the key scientific idea, area of conflict and thinking skills in each exemplar, teachers should be able to ensure a good spread of all three aspects in their teaching programme. This in turn will allow pupils the opportunity to practise and develop a range of skills.

Science process

In this publication, science process is defined as a combination of procedural understanding and the application and development of science knowledge and understanding (see table on page 12). *The National Curriculum Science Orders* identify four areas for study in investigative skills:

- planning
- obtaining and presenting evidence

- considering evidence
- evaluating.

Procedural understanding is the ability to combine all these areas of study to carry out an investigation. Usually, the more challenging aspects are drawing inferences from the evidence and evaluation and these demanding thought processes are often not well developed in pupils. Without them progress in science is diminished.

In some exemplars these aspects are explicitly identified for pupils to practise, eg drawing inferences in *Burning Candle* and in *Evaluation of an Experimental Account*. In many other exemplars the application of science knowledge and understanding is developed during group work by discussion and metacognition.

Understanding argument

It is important that pupils develop an understanding of the process of argument. This includes not only the ability to present an argument and to understand the argument of others, but also to appreciate the very bases of reasoning – such as evidence, knowledge and assumption. It is the borderland between science and philosophy. This is critical in science where much scientific knowledge comes from well-argued and substantiated claims, but it also will enable pupils to evaluate claims made in the media and associated with their everyday lives. In addition, argumentation develops pupils' language skills especially in the language of science. Well-structured activities that involve pupils developing an argument can also be linked to the ideas and evidence strand in the National Curriculum.

A recent study has shown that pupils in primary schools can engage in purposeful argument, even without training in the skills required (Naylor, Keogh and Downing, 2003). They also show good collaborative skills to arrive at a consensus. The study developed a model that is not age-related. It enables teachers to study the process of argument and pupils' participation in it and provides a useful reference for those teachers who would like to develop pupils' argumentation skills further. The skills in developing arguments are of practical value in solving problems and answering questions. Many of the situations in this publication that involve pupils' abilities to understand the process of argument begin with a key question.

In developing argument pupils should be taught to present evidence in a logical manner, taking into account the factual nature and/or interpretation of the evidence. This leads them into making a claim that is an interpretation of the evidence they have used. This claim should be clear and precise but open to discussion. It is during this discussion phase that pupils should be encouraged to question the claim. These questions could be based on issues such as errors in reasoning (eg just because one event preceded another it doesn't infer cause and effect), using unsupported evidence, or the inclusion of distractors (unrelated evidence). The questioning process enables the pupil presenting the claim to clarify her/his ideas and the pupils asking the questions to practise their questioning skills.

Pupils may choose to work in different ways to arrive at their final claim. In some instances, pupils will construct a claim by engaging in a discussion, questioning each other to arrive at an agreement (dialectic). In other situations one pupil in a group may take the lead and organise the evidence to persuade the others (rhetoric). Both of these methods are acceptable and it is worthwhile exploring, during the plenary, which method has been used. The ethos of the argument should be reasonable, thoughtful and fair. In this context, arguments can be seen to be successful even if the pupils fail to agree on the claim.

It is important that pupils understand the process in which they are engaged and it may be valuable to explain the process of argument to them before they begin. Having ground rules for engagement will enable productive arguments to be developed and some pupils will benefit from having a scaffold to help them in the process. The Key Stage 3 Strategy Foundation Subjects module *Thinking Together* is very helpful in this respect. However, teacher intervention once the argumentation has begun needs to be carefully judged to avoid inhibiting the argument. This is where class scans can be invaluable (see page 9).

Visual thinking and memory

Drawing diagrams has a long tradition in classrooms. Although it is associated with keeping pupils quiet it has far greater power, rarely fully exploited. Memory has a visuo-spatial component, which applies to both long-term memory and working memory (often referred to as the visuo-spatial sketchpad). It is interesting to note that strong parallels have been drawn between the understanding of graphics and their properties and the development of grammatical competence in children. Visual memory should be considered alongside language memory in terms of importance. Within the context of teaching thinking visual representation can be seen to have the following benefits:

1   Drawing a diagram, other than just copying, requires pupils to process or make sense of information. To produce a successful diagram pupils have to understand what they are reading, hearing or thinking about. The more complex the data, the more demanding is the transformation. There is good evidence that when individuals are instructed to use imagery in making sense of text (spoken or written) there is a powerful effect on memory. It appears that the text is dual processed as it is verbally and visually encoded so that it is more richly represented in long-term memory.

2   Diagrams are memorable especially for those with a tendency towards visualisation as a learning style. When interviewed pupils will often recall that they have visualised diagrams whilst doing exam questions. They influence retrieval from long-term memory by providing cues. Moreover these diagrams are in effect mental models which are not inert. Pupils can interrogate them, manipulate them, make inferences and apply them to new situations. Such diagrams would include storyboards, webs, concept maps, Venn diagrams, relational diagrams, cause-effect frameworks, charts, flowcharts and opinion lines. Some such diagrams are produced in exemplars in this book.

3   A diagram allows one to represent relationships in space and time with much greater clarity then when text alone is used. Experiments with university students have shown that annotated diagrams are more effective than plain text in developing understanding, as they support the structuring of knowledge.

Research about the good performance in learning map features provides some valuable pointers in the use of diagrams in a teaching thinking context (Thorndyke and Stasz, 1980). It was found that:

1   Good learners established the main lines or structure of the map and then partitioned it into areas and focused attention on one area at a time before shifting to a fresh one. Poor learners adopted a more diffuse global approach, trying to learn the whole map at once. So whether in constructing, interpreting or memorising diagrams one should be scaffolding pupils towards establishing the 'big picture' and then attending to detail in an ordered sequence.

2   Good learners reported using visuo-spatial imagery (*'it looks like a horse's head'*) to encode patterns and spatial relationships. Poor learners used no imagery and relied on verbal rehearsal of named elements or verbal mnemonics. Therefore one needs to encourage the use of a language about visual representations.

3   Good learners tested their memory to find out how they were doing and then focused on areas they had not learned. Poor learners did not do this efficiently. Therefore in the construction, interpretation and memorisation of visual forms, metacognition should be encouraged, which of course demands that pupils develop an appropriate vocabulary.

The visuo-spatial system can be fed through either direct perception (being given an image) or through the individual creating the visual image from some perceptual stimulus.

3

The Exemplars

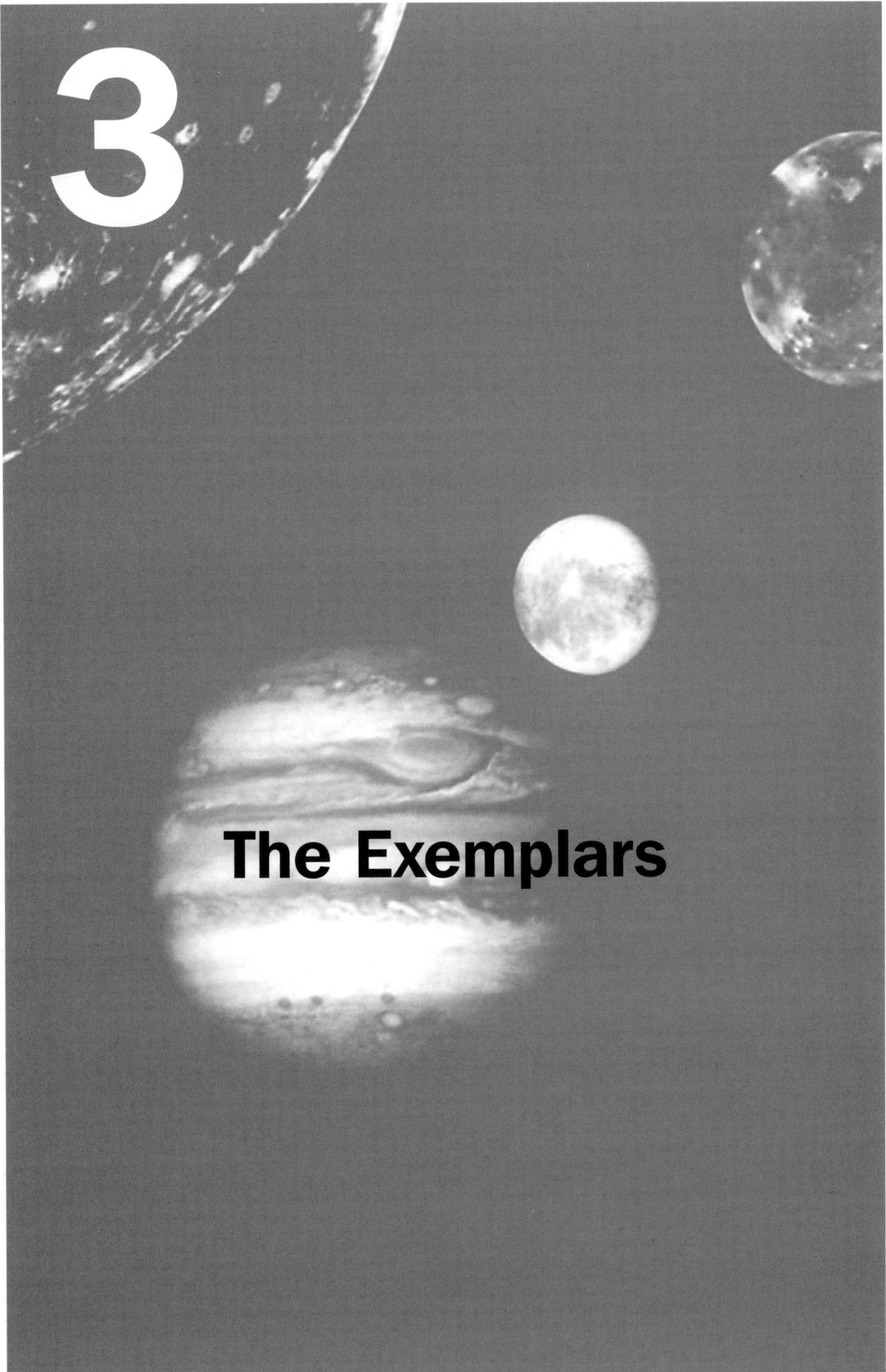

Alternative Science Theories

Outline

Science often appears to be counter-intuitive. For example, at first sight it seems logical to accept that the Sun moves across the sky, to explain the apparent movement, rather than the Earth orbits the Sun. Indeed, Lewis Wolpert has suggested that a good rule of thumb is *'if an explanation seems to be common sense then it is almost certainly scientifically wrong'*. Generally it is fairly rare to offer pupils opportunities to debate alternative theories in science lessons. This is a pity because much of the thinking to support theories is lost when alternatives are not considered.

This exemplar contains several alternative science theories that can be used together or separately. The main purpose is to offer pupils the opportunity to consider alternative theories to those that are currently widely accepted. They are offered a theory and invited to support or refute it using supporting information and logical argument. There are links to other exemplars in this book – see *What is Science?* (page 134) and *Climate Change* (page 44).

(T) This exemplar is very powerful for understanding much about the nature of argument.

Pupils' prior knowledge and skills

During Key Stage 2 pupils are taught to think creatively in order to explain how living and non-living things work, and to establish links between cause and effect. During Key Stage 3 pupils build on these ideas and are taught about the interplay between empirical questions, evidence and scientific explanations.

Links

QCA Scheme of Work	Thinking skills	Key scientific idea
Units 8C Microbes and Disease There are also links to Units 7F, 7L Units 8E, 8K Units 9A, 9H	Reasoning Creative thinking	Interdependence

Lesson objectives

Thinking skills:

- draw inferences and make deductions informed by reason and evidence
- consider alternative outcomes.

Science:

- understand the interplay between empirical questions, evidence and scientific explanations
- appreciate the predictive nature of scientific theories
- appreciate the role of creative thought in the development of scientific ideas.

Context

This activity was used with a high-attaining Year 9 set who loved it. Some of their comments included *'good lesson… you made me think'* and *'this is doing my head in!'* The activity was used about half way through the year to help pupils appreciate the importance of evidence to support theories. The class was used to small group discussions and pupils were confident about putting forward their point of view, and arguing for it.

Preparation

1 Consider how best to organise pupils in small groups to ensure effective discussion. Groups of four were found to work well.

2 Decide whether to give the same or different theories to each group. If you are doing the activity for the first time it is probably better to give all groups the same theory. This makes the plenary easier to manage.

3 For each group you will need to provide
 - a copy of your chosen alternative theory
 - paper for the group to record their answers.

4 For some groups you may wish to provide further evidence for each theory.

Introduction

1 Introduce the activity by explaining to pupils that science advances through the proposal and testing of hypotheses. You can link this to one of their own recent investigations if this is appropriate. Using an everyday example of competing theories at the beginning of the lesson helps pupils engage with the activity. (For example 'At one time people believed that the world was flat – some still do!') This approach will give pupils the confidence to tackle the more challenging areas below.

2 Alternatively, a rapid starter activity such as the following one on particles can key them into the work:

Ask pupils to respond rapidly, with observations and reasons to a set of statements that support the particle theory of matter. Pupils are usually able to do this fairly easily; and you can reinforce the need to support or refute the theory with evidence. For example 'Gases are easily compressible **because** the particles are well separated (lots of empty space)'.

3 Introduce the class to the theories, and explain carefully and clearly what they should do. Pupils should be told to consider whether a theory is acceptable or not. They will need to think of evidence that supports or refutes the theory.

4 The plenary will be easier to manage if all groups are given the same theory at the same time.

5 If you feel that pupils need some practice, you could begin by considering one theory as a class example. In one lesson with a lower-attaining group we used the theory of *Spontaneous Generation* with the whole class. An OHT of the card was used to display the theory for all. The pros and cons of the theory were discussed with the class who considered whether the evidence available supports or refutes the theory. Working in this way as a whole class helped the pupils to understand the activity more clearly before working in small groups on another theory.

In another class, the groups were given the *Dark Sucker Theory* as the sample scenario using the starter below:

'Imagine you get a biscuit tin with bright metal inside (like the posh ones at Christmas). If you go into a very bright room, put the lid on the tin and seal it with tape, then give it to someone and get them to open it in a dark room, why does the light not jump out? Where has it gone?'

6 Feedback can be structured using buzz pairs or snowballs. You may need to re-emphasise to groups that in coming to a decision about whether the theory is tenable or not they will need to consider reasons for their viewpoints. These reasons will need to be highlighted in group feedback during the plenary session.

Group work

Once group discussion started, it rapidly became animated with many pupils arguing strongly to support their beliefs. On the whole, pupils managed the conflicting claims well and were able to reach a group decision. In many cases this consisted of a judgement about the correctness of the theory with the supporting evidence. In several cases groups also presented some evidence that did not support the group decision – recognition that the evidence needed more study and discussion.

Plan the way in which you will approach the plenary during the group work session, in response to what you hear being discussed. Listening to the group deliberations will ensure that you have a variety of issues to raise in the plenary.

In some cases it became evident during the class scans that some groups were having difficulties. In these cases a brief input of evidence by the teacher moved the groups on. For example, in the case of *creative force* the teacher provided information on the relative size of a dinosaur when compared to a blue whale. This approach ensured that all groups had something to contribute to the plenary session.

(T) Strong argument is an aim of the activity.

T Consider alternative outcomes.

Feedback from the groups should be taken after about fifteen minutes. This ensures that pupils do not get stuck on one theory. It also provides an opportunity to explore the different issues raised by the other theories.

Plenary

The class scans proved useful in judging when to stop group discussion and start the plenary. The plenary was improved by making sure that pupils took the last five minutes of the discussion to prepare for feedback. In general do not wait till all groups have exhausted all reasons before stopping them. In most cases fifteen minutes was found to be adequate. The best plenaries were those where groups who supported and opposed a particular theory provided feedback in turn. This allowed groups, encouraged by the teacher, to build on earlier arguments.

T Draw inferences and make deductions informed by reason and evidence.

At the end of the session, sum up the importance of evidence in supporting or refuting hypotheses. This should also help pupils to be more aware of how science proceeds by considering and evaluating evidence. Try to make larger points about how this connects to the wider world. (For instance, the use of intelligence reports to make the case for the Iraq War were much in the news in 2003).

Follow-up

Pupils can be asked to suggest scientific enquiries that might be carried out either to support or refute the theories. Pupils could also be asked if they have heard of any other alternative theories. Some years ago an 11-year-old pupil advanced the theory of a meteorite impact on Earth causing the extinction of the dinosaurs. At the time this theory had just been reported in *New Scientist* – a fact of which the rest of the class was unaware!

References

Useful sources of information include:

- *New Scientist*, particularly 'The Last Word'.
- *Science in a Social Context*, Solomon, J., ASE/Blackwell (1983)
- *Stars and Forces*, Louis Pasteur; *The Search for Simple Substances* and *The Big Squeeze* – all in *The Nature of Science* series, Solomon, J., ASE (1989)
- The quote from Lewis Wolpert is from the BBC programme *Simple Minds*
- The rustless iron pillar has been the subject of several studies. Proposed explanations include:

    the iron is particularly pure and local conditions do not favour rusting;

    the pillar is covered with a thin layer of iron phosphate which prevents rusting. (from Wranglen, G., in *Collection of Czechoslovak Chemical Communications*, Vol.36, 625-637, 1971)

Alternative theories

Energy from the Sun

The Sun is made up mainly of coal.
It is this burning that produces the Sun's energy.

Spontaneous generation

Many living things can appear from nowhere, for example:
- if flour and sacking are placed in a barn, mice appear
- weevils just appear in ships' biscuits
- mould appears on bread
- maggots appear on dead meat

ie non-living materials make living materials.

Phlogiston

When you burn a piece of wood, most of it disappears – maybe a little ash is left. This is because the phlogiston present in the wood has escaped.

Creative force

Long ago when the world was hotter, the creative force was stronger. This gave rise to enormous dinosaurs. As the earth cooled down these died out and a weaker creative force formed the smaller modern animals in their place.

Alternative theories   PUPIL SHEET

Dark sucker theory

Light works by sucking dark. Dark is heavier than light. Dark is coloured and travels faster than light. Thus bulbs become darker over time because of all the dark they suck in. Similarly a candle has a white wick when new and this becomes black when used due to all the dark that has been sucked in.

Theory of the universe

The Earth is round and at the centre of the Universe.
The Sun, the stars and the planets all go round the Earth.
They are all carried round on invisible 'crystal spheres'.
The outermost sphere with the constellations moves fastest.

Adaptation

Lamarck believed that there is a creative force within all living animals helping them to grow stronger and larger. He realised how well animals are suited to their environment and suggested that the characteristics that they got through their struggles to survive, were passed on to their offspring, so that they became better and better adapted to their way of life eg, giraffes' necks get longer by them stretching up for food in the tree-tops.

The rustless iron pillar

This pillar at Delhi has been there for c.1500 years. In that time it has not rusted. The reason for this is either that it was made by space travellers or that the ancient Indian smiths had a secret process for stopping it rusting.

Outline

Science process is a
key focus of this exemplar.

Very often in science lessons the experimental focus is on getting experiments to work. Although it is important that pupils see the experimental justification underpinning scientific knowledge and understanding, valuable opportunities for discussing shortcomings in results and alternative explanations can be missed. In this exemplar, pupils use secondary data to gain an understanding that only part of air is used in burning and that different interpretations of the data are possible. In science it is important that pupils learn how to draw inferences and make judgements about the validity of data. An important part of scientific enquiry is to provide opportunities for pupils to order their thoughts clearly. Developing thinking skills is crucial to their science.

Pupils' prior knowledge and skills

In Key Stage 2, pupils will have experienced the idea that burning materials results in the formation of new materials. In Key Stage 3 these ideas are built on through consideration of chemical changes. Pupils also need to know the main gaseous constituents of air and that some gases dissolve in water. Some more highly-attaining pupils may also know that most materials expand on heating and contract on cooling. They may be able to use this information to think about the science process, and to explain some of the observations.

Links

QCA Scheme of Work	Thinking skills	Key scientific idea
Unit 7F Simple Chemical Reactions Units 8E, 8F	Reasoning Enquiry	Particles

Lesson objectives

Thinking skills:

- draw inferences and make deductions
- make judgements informed by reason and evidence
- predict from information provided.

Science:

- know that part of the air (oxygen) is used up during burning
- suggest and evaluate explanations.

Context

Simple experiments to show that oxygen is used up in burning are fairly straightforward, although showing the amount of oxygen used is sometimes less easy. Even when pupils are able to observe changes fairly readily and accurately, they often find it more difficult to explain what is happening, particularly where there are several steps in the argument. This exemplar is designed to fit in with the Year 7 QCA Scheme of Work (and has been used successfully with Year 7), but in this case it was used with Year 8 groups who had not experienced it before.

The activity was carried out with two Year 8 classes, one with high prior attainment and the other with lower prior attainment. It was used as a consolidation activity towards the end of the academic year to reinforce science knowledge and understanding as well as to improve pupils' reasoning skills. Both classes were used to having small group discussions during their science lessons. Generally this way of working has improved the quality of pupils' answers, involved more members of the class and encouraged pupils to be less concerned with providing what they see as the 'right' answers. This lesson lasted 50 minutes and pupils enjoyed the task. For one of the classes involved it turned out to be one of the best activities for getting pupils involved and thinking through their work. The exemplar was run as a written task in small groups with the higher-attaining group as presented below. With the lower-attaining group, the activity worked better when questions 1 and 2 were run as a discussion with pupils as a whole class, followed by a discussion of questions 3 and 4 in small groups. (see page 35)

For pupils who are having difficulty, a crib sheet or a series of prompt cards may be helpful. Examples are given on page 36 – but you can create your own.

Alternatively, questions based on the QCA Scheme of Work 'What is needed for things to burn' (Unit 7F, p4) could be used.

Preparation

1 Organise pupils into groups: threes or fours are probably best. In the lesson described, pupils were allowed to choose their own groups and this worked well with a good level of animated discussion.

2 This activity can be linked to the erroneous idea found in some older textbooks that 'the candle in a bell jar' experiment shows that c. 20% of the air is oxygen. The experiment is a nice example of something that almost 'works' but for the wrong reason. In a sense the experiment appears deceptively simple.

3 The prompt cards are useful if pupils need some help to get going.

4 You will need
   - sufficient copies of the QUESTIONS sheet – one per group
   - sufficient copies of the PROMPT CARDS, if you feel that they would help.

The main emphasis of this activity is on explaining what is happening, supported by evidence and argument, based on observation (enquiry skills).

> Links to ideas and evidence in Sc1.

> Some points to note:
> - Gas can escape from the bottom of the jar.
> - Not all the oxygen is used up.
> - Some carbon dioxide will dissolve in the water.

Introduction

1 It is always a good idea to tune pupils in to a lesson and these two starter activities have been used successfully:
   - A starter activity, which has worked well with a more able group, is a quick question and answer session about gases in the air, the effect of heating and cooling and what happens when things burn. This needs to be kept brief, to the point and be pacey.
   - You can carry out a teacher demonstration of the process with appropriate discussion. Adding food colouring to the water helps pupils see the change in level. If you choose to do this you will need a large glass container, a trough for the water, and a lighted candle on a piece of cork. **There is no need for the pupils to perform the experiment.**

2 After the starter activity, introduce the task to pupils by using and explaining the diagram on the *Questions for group discussion* worksheet, drawing attention to the key changes taking place. It is important that the introduction is clear and that pupils agree about the observations. Explain the task. Make sure they understand what they have to do (answer the questions on the worksheet as a group – through discussion with each other) and how long they have to do it. Explain that you do not expect them to ask you questions about how to carry out the activity once they have started. If they get stuck prompt cards are available.

3 Pupils should work in groups of three or four to answer the questions. Emphasise the need for discussion and debate so as to provide reasons for the answers they give. Each group should record their answers and reasons on the group recording sheet.

> (T) Prior knowledge can be determined from the starter activity and used for assessment.

> (T) Direct observations helped some pupils to grasp more clearly what was happening.

> (T) A good quality overhead transparency of the diagram on the worksheet is useful here. PowerPoint and interactive whiteboards can also be used to good effect. BUT keep the focus on the thinking.

Group work

The classes found the activity worthwhile and enjoyable. There was a good level of debate within most groups about exactly what was going on and why. Some were unsure of the meaning of flawed (question 3) and valid (question 4) in this context. As expected, question 4 posed the greatest challenge to pupils.

The prompt cards may help pupils who are having real difficulty with answering the questions. They provide the necessary sharper focus for discussion without giving the answer. For example, the 'translation' of the word equation both helps in the general understanding of word equations as well as giving information that helps pupils give an answer to the question.

Carry out a class scan as the pupils work. Notes of what pupils say and do may be useful. If the broad outcomes from each group are known, this will help in managing the plenary.

> (T) Language development.

> (T) Predict from information provided.

Contributions from each group can be managed and therefore valued in the plenary. It is important not to get drawn into discussion with groups. If they have a problem encourage them to talk to one another, ask open-ended questions or use the prompt cards, as appropriate. Keep an eye on the progress of all groups.

It is probably better to stop the group work early once at least one group has finished rather than allow early finishers to go off task. After all, one contribution from each group to the plenary will satisfy the aims of the exercise.

Plenary

It is important to ensure that you leave sufficient time for a quality session here. Knowing what each group has found out (from class scans), you can take feedback from each group in turn. Start with the group that found out least, and then in order, ending with the group that has the best understanding of findings. Each group needs time to give their answers as well as to explain their reasoning. Note the key findings, rationales and explanations. Use any disagreements between groups constructively to develop pupils' skills of logic and argument to make links to the overarching framework of scientific enquiry.

> (T) Reasoning skills.

> (T) Draw inferences and make deductions.

> (T) Make judgements informed by reasons and evidence.

Most groups in the higher-attaining class discussed questions 1 and 2 well, but about half the class ran into trouble with questions 3 and 4. With a lower-attaining group, you may find that completing questions 1 and 2 as a class discussion, emphasising the importance of the reasoning involved, helps to tackle the last two questions with the aid of the prompt cards. Thus the hints in question 3 (oxygen used up and carbon dioxide produced) may help pupils to work out that the volume change is not only the result of the oxygen being used up. You may wish to record key points to which pupils can refer or include this in other work on simple reactions.

> (T) This is a good example of the need to accept that getting right answers to all the questions is not the aim - thinking hard is the whole point.

Follow-up

Suitable activities can be found in the AKSIS publications listed in the reference section.

References

- *AKSIS Investigations – Getting to Grips with Graphs*, Goldsworthy, A., Watson, R. and Wood-Robinson, V., ASE (1999) 086 357 3029. Activity 13 could be used in conjunction with this exemplar. It looks at time taken for a candle to be extinguished in different sized containers.
- *AKSIS Investigations – Developing Understanding*, Goldsworthy, A., Watson, R. and Wood-Robinson, V., ASE (2000) 086 357 310X. Activity 21 could be used to extend this activity 'phlogiston theory' 7F,8E, 8F, 9E, 9F.
- *From Phlogiston to Oxygen*, ASE, 0 86357 317 7
- *Children's Learning in Science Project, Workshop No 3*, HMSO (1990)

Questions for group discussion

PUPIL SHEET

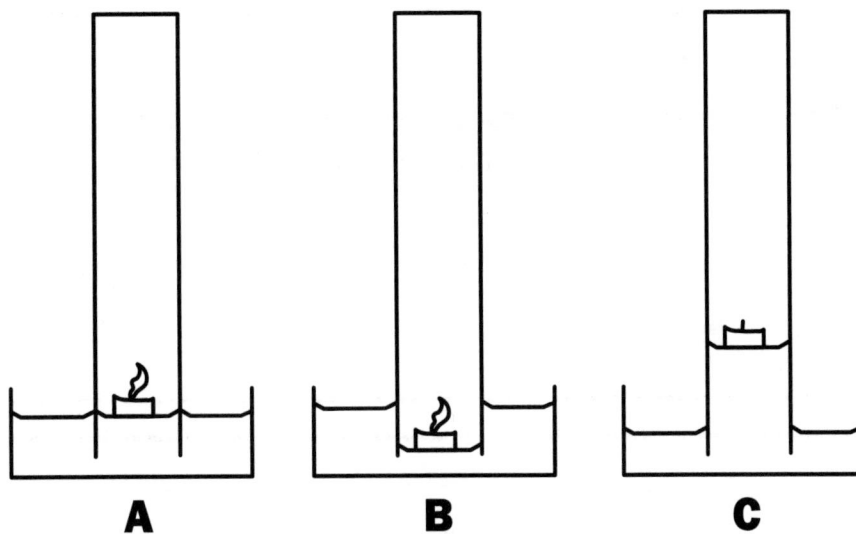

A **B** **C**

What happens?
- The apparatus was set up as shown in diagram A with the candle lit.
- Initially the water level falls as shown in diagram B.
- Eventually the candle goes out and the water level rises as shown in diagram C.

Discussion

1 What is present in the jar at the start of the experiment?

---

2 The reaction can be summarised by: hydrocarbon (candle) + oxygen → carbon dioxide + water

- What is used up as the candle burns?

- What is produced as the candle burns?

- Why does the water level fall initially?

- Why does the water level rise after the candle has gone out?

---

3 In some older textbooks this experiment was used to try to show that air was made up of c. 20% oxygen. Why is this explanation flawed?

---

4 This experiment can be used to demonstrate the approximate proportion of oxygen in air, by replacing the candle with another substance.

- If the experiment is to be valid, what state do the products of burning need to end up in, and why?

- Can you suggest a suitable substance? Justify your choice.

Prompt cards

PROMPT 1
The 'jar' was taken off the laboratory bench before inverting it over the trough.
Thus which ONE of the following best describes the contents of the jar?

Air

Hydrogen

Oxygen

Nitrogen.

PROMPT 2
Translated, the word equation says 'When the candle burns it reacts with oxygen (in the air) to produce carbon dioxide, gas and water (vapour)'.

PROMPT 3
Materials expand on heating.

PROMPT 4
When cooled, materials contract.

PROMPT 5
Oxygen gas is used up. Carbon dioxide gas is produced.

PROMPT 6
For equal masses, gases take up a much greater volume than solids or liquids.

Outline

This exemplar contains two activities that can be taught separately or linked.

- A sequencing activity where pupils arrange the cards about the carbon cycle to show how they are linked.
- An imaginative/creative thinking activity where pupils imagine that they are a carbon atom, and describe their journey through any part of the cycle. This can be in prose form (using ICT if wished), a poem or a poster and could be produced individually or as a group. The Activity could also be acted out. This might benefit kinaesthetic learners.

> (T) The transformation of data and visual presentation of the carbon cycle support understanding.

Pupils' prior knowledge and skills

The carbon cycle is not specifically mentioned at Key Stage 3. Nonetheless many of its component parts and processes are referred to in the key stage, such as feeding, respiration and decay, geological changes, combustion and other chemical reactions.

Links

> The exemplar has links with literacy in science in both activities.

QCA Scheme of Work	Thinking skills	Key scientific idea
No specific link overall Units which address parts include 7F,7I,7L,8A,8B,8G,9B,9D,9E,9G,9H	Reasoning Information processing Creative thinking	Interdependence

Lesson objectives

Thinking skills:

- make judgements informed by reason and evidence
- use information to sequence processes
- apply imagination.

Science:

- appreciate the interdependence of plants, animals, the atmosphere, lithosphere and the hydrosphere
- know that carbon cycles through the system
- know the names for the relevant processes.

Context

This exemplar provides a useful way of linking different parts of the Key Stage 3 programme of study, and as such can provide a different type of overview of the importance of carbon. Thus it could provide a useful and challenging form of revision of known material (but in a new context) as well as a good preparation for (and lead into) Key Stage 4. The exemplar was used with two top-ability Year 9 groups towards the end of the summer term, after the Key Stage 3 tests. In these lessons pupils got very involved with the activity and discussed, argued and formulated a variety of carbon cycles. The activity was a stimulating one after the tests but could equally well be used as a revision exercise before the tests. One of the groups, pleased with their result, decided to produce a poster of their answer. They displayed this in the laboratory where it created considerable interest and debate within other science classes. Lower-attaining groups were also successful with the activity when the number of cards was limited (for example, using only atmospheric carbon dioxide, animals, herbivores and plants as the component cards). Some pupils tended to produce a linear progression rather than a cycle and needed guidance to close the loop.

> Standard texts contain a range of slightly different carbon cycles.

> Colour coding the two sets of cards makes it easier for pupils to distinguish between the constituent and process cards as does 'defining' the meaning of the two.

Preparation

Activity 1: Sequencing – arranging cards

1 You need to assess the prior attainment of pupils in the class and whether you should limit the cards to which they have access.

2 Allocate pupils to groups.

3   Photocopy the cards and cut up. Put them into sets – one for each group.

4   During the activity the cards can be fixed to a large sheet of paper using Blu-tack (or Velcro) to make a semi-permanent display. This is useful for reference during the plenary.

Activity 2: Imagine you are a carbon atom

1   Pupils may use all or part of the sequenced carbon cycle they have produced in Activity 1, or you can produce a simple cycle for them and photocopy it.

2   Again, depending on the prior attainment of the pupils in each group, the level of difficulty will be readily differentiated by task if they use their own cycles, as the more able pupils will involve more processes and transformations in the carbon cycle they produce.

3   You may wish to discuss with some groups the number of transformations that they attempt to include. Or, as above, you can provide some groups with a simple pre-prepared cycle.

4   For higher-attaining pupils, additional points such as sub-sea vents, volcanoes and subduction can be considered. More cards will be needed if this is the case (you can make them, or get the pupils to make their own).

> Laminating the cards for long-term use is cost effective and improves their appearance.

Introduction

One way to get started is to say *'So you know quite a lot about carbon then…'*, getting a few pupils to tell the group one thing they know. Then, challenge the group to show how this information can be set out differently to show the inter-relationships.

> Using the water cycle as an example of a **cycle** helped pupils who were sequencing directly.

Activity 1: Sequencing – arranging cards

Introduce sequencing by explaining to pupils that they are to arrange all the cards in an order which shows how carbon cycles through the environment. The *process* cards should be placed between the appropriate *constituent* cards. If they are to be using ALL the cards (rather than a selection) you need to emphasise that they should use as many cards as possible. It may help some pupils if you show them a simple example as an indication of the expected outcome. Emphasise the importance of working as a group and explain that the final arrangement or sequence must be supported by reasoning and agreement.

Activity 2: Imagine you are a carbon atom

This is an imaginative/creative thinking activity, so you will need to stress the importance of the application of imagination, ie what the experience would be like, as well as the use of scientific accuracy. They can use all or part of their own cycle (or a pre-prepared cycle) as the basis of the journey. Pupils should visualise themselves as small atoms moving through the cycle. It helps if you act this out for an obvious section of the cycle. For combustion, say:

> Pupils need to be clear about all aspects of the task before they start group work.

> *'I am vibrating about in a lump of coal. Suddenly, it gets warmer and warmer. I start to move faster. My friends above suddenly disappear as they move off the surface of the lump of coal and I am met by lots of molecules of oxygen. I jump off with them, holding their hands and become part of a carbon dioxide molecule. This is hot work. I am sweating. As the heat gets less, I find myself flying though the clear blue sky. However, I am much heavier now that I have these two new oxygen friends and find this flying hard work.'*

It may be worthwhile explaining the relative size of atoms at this point and pointing out that they need to imagine being little carbon atoms. The practical details of what the expected outcomes are need to be made clear to pupils. Do you expect a prose or word-processed document, or indeed a 'mini-play'? Or you may wish some groups to produce a poster, poem or even a sketch or picture (possibly additionally as homework).

> It is important that you emphasise to pupils, where you feel it necessary, that although this process may ask them to visualise themselves as little atoms, in fact atoms are not alive, cannot make decisions or do things as a result of conscious thought – nor indeed do they have feelings!

Group work

Activity 1: Sequencing – arranging cards

Pupils worked in groups of three or four. Once they had understood the need to set up a cycle, effective discussion took place. An introduction in which part of the water cycle was demonstrated helped to cue pupils into the task. Moving cards about also aided discussion. Note the various group responses by class scans during the group work to help in managing the plenary, and encourage groups to agree a collective final cycle. The cycles which the groups produced provided a useful reminder of some of the discussions that took place.

Activity 2: Imagine you are a carbon atom

Groups worked on the cycles and produced an imaginative product in the agreed form (story, poster etc). In most cases they enjoyed this and stayed on task well. One group even produced an audio- tape of the journey! The task stimulated the pupils' imagination – particularly when organised into groups where those with more imagination were able to steer the others.

Plenary

Activity 1: Sequencing – arranging cards

One or two groups had not finalised their version of the cycle when group work was stopped. These were chosen to feed back first, then the other groups in turn so that all pupils had an opportunity to contribute to the process and develop their thinking skills beyond the level at which they were working. The final cycles produced by groups acted as a visual prompt to enable each group to explain aspects of their deliberations during the plenary. Once the groups have presented their work (including explaining the thinking behind it), the posters were displayed on the wall and groups were invited to challenge one another over the differences. This led to further discussion with an eventual consensus 'best answer' emerging.

Activity 2: Imagine you are a carbon atom

Pupils shared their writing by reading their work to the rest of the class, and the writing was displayed in the laboratory. Pupils were encouraged to discuss their work with one another. The displays acted as a useful focus for other groups who were invited to comment on them or pose questions. The group that had produced the audio-tape played it to the class who listened attentively, finishing off with a round of applause.

Follow-up

Possible links to the wider issues of carbon in the environment include time scales, role of oceans, volcanic activity, explanation of global warming with reference to the carbon cycle and possible solutions, subduction etc. Devising and making simple board games is another possibility that pupils might develop.

References

Earth Story, Lamb and Sington, BBC Books, 0563 38799 8

T Use information to sequence processes.

T Apply imagination.

T Be able to make judgements informed by reason and evidence.

T This process generated the hardest thinking and shows the value of collective thinking.

Possible links here to geography, eg issues of sustainability.

Thinking Skills Through Science

PROCESSES in the carbon cycle   PUPIL SHEET

PROCESS Feeding	PROCESS Decomposing
PROCESS Dissolves in water, attacks rocks, and soluble materials washed into the sea	PROCESS Respiration
PROCESS Sedimentation of shells	PROCESS Heat
PROCESS Combustion	PROCESS Decay and great pressure
PROCESS Photosynthesis	PROCESS Respiration and decay

CONSTITUENT PARTS of the carbon cycle PUPIL SHEET

CONSTITUENT Plants	CONSTITUENT Animals
CONSTITUENT Chalk/limestone	CONSTITUENT Carbon in excreted materials
CONSTITUENT Atmospheric carbon dioxide	CONSTITUENT Herbivores
CONSTITUENT Carnivores	CONSTITUENT Fuels (oil, natural gas, coal)

Sc1.1a. The interplay between empirical questions, evidence and scientific explanations.

Outline

Many pupils view science as an activity carried out by men in white coats doing experiments to get the 'right' answer, rather than seeing science as a way of thinking. By taking a very topical issue this exemplar represents science as a subject where contested value-ridden views abound, evidence is conflicting, firm conclusions are difficult to reach, and where a controlled experiment is not really possible. In other words, school science does not really reflect what some scientists do.

This exemplar focuses on ideas and evidence in science and allows pupils to consider and evaluate evidence about a topical science issue – global warming. It provides an opportunity for pupils to appreciate that science is always developing and that not all that happens is fully understood. The consequence of this is that natural systems are complex, causal effects are not always easy to establish and simple definitive answers are not available. The exemplar may be used as a follow on to other exemplars: *What is Science?* (page 134) and *Alternative Science Theories* (page 26). It provides pupils with an opportunity to evaluate statements about climate change. Pupils answer the question *'Is the human race responsible for climate change in the twentieth and twenty-first centuries?'*

There are two stages to the investigation. The first activity involves a discussion where pupils consider the widely accepted facts in order to come to a judgement about whether or not we are responsible for climate change. This can be followed by a second discussion which encourages pupils to develop theories of what may happen. As a result pupils should have a greater understanding of the complexities of climate change. This will provide pupils with the opportunity to appreciate how scientific theories develop, the uncertainties involved and the existence of vested interests.

Evidence is provided under three headings:

- widely accepted facts
- what is likely to happen
- uncertainties.

Pupils' prior knowledge and skills

During Key Stage 2 pupils will have had opportunities to test ideas using evidence from observation and measurement. They will also have checked conclusions against their earlier predictions. These skills will have been further developed in Key Stage 3. Pupils will almost certainly be aware of the concerns over global warming, although probably less certain about its causes and full effects.

Links

QCA Scheme of Work	Thinking skills	Key scientific idea
Unit 9G Environmental Chemistry	Reasoning Evaluation	Interdependence

Lesson objectives

Thinking skills:

- make judgements and decisions informed by evidence
- make deductions
- evaluate information
- develop criteria for judging the value of information.

Science:

- how to decide whether evidence is good enough to answer a question
- evaluate evidence put forward by others
- discuss and evaluate conflicting evidence to arrive at a considered viewpoint.

Context

This lesson was carried out with four Year 9 classes. One was a high-attaining group, one a low-attaining group and the other two were middle-ability groups. Almost all the pupils involved were aware of the term *global warming* and their work on the Environmental Chemistry unit 9G from the QCA Scheme of Work was used as a basis for this exemplar. All groups engaged well. They identified with the issue, and were able to draw on evidence from their previous work. Where groups had previously carried out the *What is Science?* exemplar, they were able to link their findings to the work in this activity. This enabled them to identify how evidence can be used to develop a more secure theory.

Preparation

1 If you are uncertain about aspects of global warming, eg the *'North Atlantic Oscillation'*, you will find the reference books listed helpful (see page 47).

2 The exemplar can be an intellectually challenging activity. You can adjust the difficulty by restricting the number and/or complexity of the statements given to groups. Make a decision about this based on your knowledge of the pupils in the class. Similarly you will need to consider group composition carefully to ensure an effective outcome.

3 Photocopy the statements and cut them up. Decide which of the statements to use, and separate them into envelopes labelled *Widely Accepted Facts, What is Likely to Happen?* and *Uncertainties*.

4 Organise pupils in groups of three or four. Give each group a copy of the five *Key Scientific Points*.

Introduction

1 If pupils have just finished a unit such as 9G they will need little cueing into the activity. For example, asking them if they can recall one fact about climate changes over time should be sufficient to generate an enthusiastic and informed response. If they have not done 9G, a simple question such as *'If glaciers melt, the sea level will rise. How might I be affected by these sea level changes if I live on the coast?'* would be a useful starting point.

2 Give pupils the question: *'Is the human race responsible for climate change in the twentieth and twenty-first centuries?'* Write it on the board.

3 Draw pupils' attention to the five *Key Scientific Points* using a flip chart or overhead projector. Give pupils the cards *Widely Accepted Facts*. You will need to explain that the *Widely Accepted Facts* are just that – facts, not clear evidence of a causal link. You may wish to amplify this last point by drawing on pupils' experience of listening to people on TV and radio who talk about an issue and say *'The facts are…'*. Invariably there is someone else who disagrees and often there is no clear outcome. Facts on their own are rarely enough – they need to be interpreted. (And what is a fact anyway?) The best we can do sometimes is to keep an open mind and check our assumptions. You may wish to ask pupils to define a fact or give an example of a fact to reinforce the point.

4 Pupils should select from the fact cards those that support or refute the question. In considering the *Widely Accepted Facts* encourage pupils to back up their conclusions with evidence from what they know as well as the information provided on the cards.

5 For the second activity give out the two sets of cards *What is Likely to Happen?* and *Uncertainties* to each group. Ask pupils to form predictions based on the available information, taking into account the uncertainties associated with these predictions. They should select one or two predictions that are linked, suggest possible causes for these which are related to human activity, and indicate the relevant uncertainties. It may be helpful to classify the uncertainties as: *important; not important and don't know*. They could also be encouraged to suggest what might be done to reduce the uncertainties.

6 Pupils need to be sure about what they have to do before moving to the group work for each of the activities. It is probably better to deal with the two activities one at a time. The group work and plenary paragraphs which follow assume two separate activities.

> (T) An alternative approach is to provide pupils with a mix of the statements asking them to classify them as facts, uncertainties etc. In this case, the headings will need to be omitted. Again they will need to give reasons for their decisions. This should lead to lively debate about evidence, deductions and evaluation.

> (T) Evaluate evidence and information.

Group work

During the discussions you will need to carry out a class scan (and possibly make notes) to check whether there are any major differences between groups that can be used in the plenary session. It is important not to get drawn into discussion with groups. If they have a problem encourage them to talk to one another. It is probably easiest to take feedback on the first discussion (first plenary) before moving on to the second discussion and a second plenary.

First activity

In one class a group of pupils were able to advance the following arguments:

- evidence of global warming:
    - global temperature rise;
    - a rise in sea level;
    - 5 of 6 warmest years since records began have been since 1989.
- caused by greenhouse effect:
    - increase in greenhouse gases, carbon dioxide, methane and water vapour.
- industrial activities have increased production of these.
- thus human activity is responsible for global warming.
- BUT particulates from industrial activity produce a cooling effect.

Another group advanced the view that although it looked as if humans were responsible for global warming, the key points indicated that there was insufficient evidence to come to a firm conclusion.

Second activity

Where classes coped well with the first activity they were moved on to the second activity.

Using the cards *What is Likely to Happen?* and *Uncertainties*, pupils need to come up with a view as to the most likely scenario, taking into account the uncertainties. Groups can produce a brief written statement outlining their view. Manage the group work to ensure that all groups have covered both aspects: *'What is Likely to Happen?'* and *'Uncertainties'*.

You may well have to field questions about flipping systems. Or get pupils to research these, either through available reference material or from websites. This could also form part of an integrated homework. As before, carry out class scans and then take feedback (second plenary).

Plenary

As indicated above, this is probably best managed in two parts, the first dealing with whether the human race is responsible for global warming (first activity), and the second looking at what might happen and the attendant uncertainties (second activity). Careful observation during discussion helps the management of the plenary. Take the feedback from each group to identify common areas of uncertainty or conflict.

First plenary

Generally most pupils judge that global warming is taking place. However, their views on the supporting evidence are often less clear. In the above example, the first plenary discussion became quite heated when pupils brought to bear their first hand experience of scientific enquiry on the strength of the evidence to support or refute global warming – particularly the effect of the activities of the human race.

Second plenary

The second plenary highlights different predictions for the future. It is important to get the groups to explain their reasoning for this: many variables; data over a relatively short period; a variety of uncertainties; and vested interests – climatologists as well as big business, etc. The main outcome was that most pupils agreed that there is global warming. Their principal evidence was the break up of the Larsen B ice-shelf in March 2002. What was less clear were the reasons for this, though increasingly carbon dioxide emissions look to be a contributory factor. At the end of the lesson many pupils had come to appreciate the complexity of the issue. Not only had they begun to realise that evidence does not always point in just one direction, but also that there are a number of competing and inter-related factors affecting the system.

(T) 'The Precautionary Principle' may be worth mentioning, ie you might think differently if the consequences of something are difficult to reverse and are severe.

For a brief explanation of flipping systems see *'The Blue Planet.'*

(T) Make judgements and decisions informed by evidence.

(T) Develop criteria for judging the value of information.

(T) Make deductions.

Follow-up

Pupils can carry out further research on climate change and its possible effects through newspaper articles and web sites.

References

- *Climate Change – Scientific Certainties and Uncertainties,* National Environment Research Council, October 2000
- *Earth Story*, Lamb & Sington, BBC Books, 0563 38799 8
- *Blue Planet*, Byatt, Fothergill & Holmes, BBC Books, 2001
- *New Scientist* and some newspapers have regular updates on global warming

(T) The handling of issues where there is no right answer is an important part of inducting pupils into the world of real science.

Key scientific points

PUPIL SHEET

1

KEY POINT

Studies of sediments and ice cores show that in the past the climate has swung between cold and warm conditions.

2

KEY POINT

The earth's climate is maintained through interactions between the atmosphere, oceans, ice and land surface.

3

KEY POINT

At present evidence is gathering that the earth is warming and that human activities accelerate this.

4

KEY POINT

Sometimes these changes have been slow, at other times abrupt.

5

KEY POINT

Climate change is perhaps the most pressing and urgent environmental issue on the World's agenda.

Widely accepted facts

1

FACT

Average global temperature has risen by 0.6 °C in the last 140 years.

2

FACT

Carbon dioxide, methane and nitrous oxide levels are rising mainly as a result of human activities.

3

FACT

Methane levels in the atmosphere have doubled over the last 100 years.

4

FACT

Five of the six warmest years in Central England have occurred since 1989 (records go back for 340 years).

5

FACT

Carbon dioxide levels in the atmosphere have risen by about 32% in the last 200 years.

6

FACT

Global sea level has risen by 10 - 25 cm over the last 100 years.

Widely accepted facts

PUPIL SHEET

FACT 7

Ozone has a complex effect. Close to the Earth's surface increased levels of ozone leads to warming. But ozone depletion has a cooling effect.

FACT 8

Oceans redistribute heat globally via their circulation patterns.

FACT 9

Oceans are particularly important as they act as giant heat reservoirs.

FACT 10

It is thought that tiny particles in the atmosphere reflect sunlight and produce a cooling effect, eg volcanic eruptions and industrial activities.

FACT 11

Carbon dioxide, methane, nitrous oxide and water vapour are all greenhouse gases.

FACT 12

Greenhouse gases trap radiation emitted from the earth's surface, keeping the earth about 30°C warmer than it otherwise would be.

What is likely to happen?

1 WHAT MIGHT HAPPEN? The rise in temperature produces an impact on a wide range of climate related features.	**2** WHAT MIGHT HAPPEN? Weather will become more extreme - heat waves, droughts, floods.
3 WHAT MIGHT HAPPEN? If greenhouse gas emissions continue to increase at the current levels, there will be a temperature rise of 1.5 - 5.5°C by 2100.	**4** WHAT MIGHT HAPPEN? The world's vegetation zones undergo major change.
5 WHAT MIGHT HAPPEN? Global sea levels rise by 20 - 90cm over the next 100 years.	**6** WHAT MIGHT HAPPEN? Half the world's glaciers melt.

What is likely to happen?

7

WHAT MIGHT
HAPPEN?

Agricultural productivity
varies more widely.

8

WHAT MIGHT
HAPPEN?

Diseases spread to new areas,
eg malaria in the UK.

9

WHAT MIGHT
HAPPEN?

Conflict over water
resources increases.

10

WHAT MIGHT
HAPPEN?

Decreasing ice cover leads to
increased temperatures.

11

WHAT MIGHT
HAPPEN?

Mass movement of
people occurs due to
floods and famine.

Uncertainties

PUPIL SHEET

1

UNCERTAINTY ABOUT THE FACTS

Scientists are not sure how carbon moves between the soil, rocks, oceans and atmosphere.

2

UNCERTAINTY ABOUT THE FACTS

Solar radiation varies and we are unsure about significant variation over long periods of time and its effect.

3

UNCERTAINTY ABOUT THE FACTS

Temperatures fluctuate from year to year and over much longer timescales. Accurate records only exist for about a century so identifying small changes against background variation is difficult.

4

UNCERTAINTY ABOUT THE FACTS

Sea temperatures are greatly influenced by what goes on deep in the ocean and effects are not predictable.

5

UNCERTAINTY ABOUT THE FACTS

Tiny particles in the atmosphere can cause either heating or cooling.

Uncertainties

1

UNCERTAINTY ABOUT FEEDBACK

The effect of clouds is twofold – they can reflect incoming radiation into space but they can also prevent surface radiation escaping into space. What happens depends on the height, temperature and properties of the clouds.

2

UNCERTAINTY ABOUT FEEDBACK

Absorption of solar radiation may change as ice sheets melt and darker surfaces are present.

3

UNCERTAINTY ABOUT FEEDBACK

If carbon dioxide levels increase plant growth may increase, hence absorbing more carbon from the atmosphere – negative feedback.

4

UNCERTAINTY ABOUT FEEDBACK

Polar ice sheets melt as temperature rises but snowfall may increase.

5

UNCERTAINTY ABOUT FEEDBACK

Water vapour is a powerful greenhouse gas: a warmer atmosphere can hold more water vapour thus amplifying warming by positive feedback.

Uncertainties

1

UNCERTAINTY
ABOUT FLIPPING
SYSTEMS

'The North Atlantic
Oscillation'

2

UNCERTAINTY
ABOUT FLIPPING
SYSTEMS

'The Atlantic Conveyor'

3

UNCERTAINTY
ABOUT FLIPPING
SYSTEMS

'El Nino'

Outline

Being required to reproduce a complex diagram is a powerful aid to developing pupils' understanding. This exemplar develops pupils' visual memory as well as their awareness of different strategies they can use for memorising information. Working in groups, pupils are required to reproduce a diagram of the digestive system. In order to successfully complete the task, pupils need to decide on a collaborative system for transmitting information from a whole class diagram to their group diagram. The purpose of the activity is to encourage pupils to devise and carry out a strategy to collect and reproduce the information. By working in groups, pupils can support and learn from each other. This is particularly important for less able pupils or those who lack confidence. Introducing an element of competition works well for some pupils.

Pupils' prior knowledge and skills

Pupils need no prior knowledge of the digestive system. Indeed it may be better that they have no prior knowledge of the structure of the alimentary canal, in order to develop their thinking.

Links

QCA Scheme of Work	Thinking skills	Key scientific idea
Unit 8A Food and Digestion	Creative thinking	Cells

Lesson objectives

Thinking skills:

- devise a creative strategy to solve a problem.

Science:

- know the organisation of the organs of the digestive system.

Context

Diagrams form an integral part of science lessons and play an important role in pupils' understanding of science concepts. The most frequent uses of diagrams are:

- representations, often in a simplified manner, of systems not easily accessible or visible to pupils. Examples include organ systems in living (or ex-living!) organisms, and very small or very large structures such as cells or blast furnaces.
- simplified diagrammatic representations such as circuit diagrams.
- to make science accessible to pupils whose preferred learning style is visual.

Diagrams can be used to help pupils understand structures such as that of a cell, or they can be used to aid understanding of function, such as the function of spectacles to correct long or short sight. Pupils' knowledge and understanding can be determined by using the drawing or labelling of diagrams as an assessment tool. Pupils often need to recall and draw diagrams in external tests and examinations. They may also be required to label diagrams provided for them. In the case of circuit diagrams, not only will they need to be able to recall the symbols for the individual components but they also need to know how to construct a circuit diagram.

In some lessons, pupils can copy diagrams with very little thinking involved! Sometimes this is demonstrated by an inaccurate drawing, but beware that if the pupil is skilled in copying and takes pride in presentation this will not be apparent from the finished product.

This exemplar was first carried out with a middle-ability class of Year 8 pupils. They had done no work on the structure of the digestive system, although most knew the names of the main organs and some recalled that they had done something about this in primary school. They were not told that the diagram was of the digestive system before the activity was carried out. The lesson was very successful and was repeated with a less able group who found the activity much more challenging. Their poor drawing skills and lack of confidence impeded their involvement initially.

Preparation

1 You will need to have at least one (and preferably two) diagrams of the digestive system (see page 59) copied onto a large piece of paper. The number you need depends on the number of groups in the class and the ease of accessibility in the classroom. Have at least one diagram for every four groups, especially if there is an element of competition in the activity. Any more than four pupils trying to get a look at the diagram can cause over-enthusiastic crowding. The diagrams are laid flat on the teacher's bench at the front and out of general sight of the pupils.

2 Each group will need a large blank piece of paper, preferably slightly smaller than the original, and drawing instruments, pencils, rubbers etc.

> When the diagrams are used several times they can become dog-eared and the printing can become less clear. If you are planning to reuse them, protect the surface in some way such as with clear plastic or lamination.

Introduction

1 If pupils have not done this type of activity before you need to make the expected outcomes very clear. Rules should be explained. You need to control the timing very carefully.

2 Introduce the activity with an attention-grabbing example, preferably something that will enable pupils to see the relevance of the activity in their everyday lives. For example, this activity is useful for devising strategies to help you visualise something that is quite complicated, like finding the route to a new place: '*If I'd been able to visualise the route I had to drive to find the restaurant where I'd agreed to meet my friends, I'd never have been late because I wouldn't have got lost – and my friends would still be speaking to me.*'

> The activity requires pupils to work in groups. The best number appears to be three. If the number of pupils in the class is not divisible by three, then larger numbers work better than pairs.

3 Explain that each group has to decide on a collaborative system for transmitting the information from a central diagram to the group diagram. Pupils have to visit in turn the diagram on the teacher's bench, and reproduce the diagram as faithfully as possible onto their group sheet. It helps if you don't tell them what the diagram is. This way they have to concentrate on working out the strategy they will use at the outset. If they are told first, pupils who think they already know the answer may try drawing before working out a strategy for memorising.

4 Pupils will produce one collaborative diagram per group. The rules are:

- Pupils will not be told of the content of the diagram before the first visit to the teacher's bench.
- Pupils have to decide on the strategy to use beforehand, and should make a note of each person's task and any subsequent changes to their strategy. Groups will be given 5 minutes planning time before the visits begin.
- Only one person at a time from each group can go to the front to look at the diagram on the teacher's bench.
- Each pupil will have 10 seconds per visit to look at the diagram but they are **not allowed** to take notes.
- Each pupil is allowed a maximum of 2 visits – the teacher will be looking for the most successful group in the minimum amount of time.

5 Groups must be prepared to explain their strategy during the plenary.

Group work

Timing pupils' visits to look at the diagram, while the rest of each group carries out the task needs careful management. Allow plenty of time and encouragement for pupils to plan a strategy and to be able to articulate their decisions. Using the following prompts will help:

- Work out the order the group will visit the diagram.

- Will individuals be required to remember as much as they can at each visit, each deciding how much to do?

- Will the first person try to get an outline, and leave others to fill in the detail? If so, how will the subsequent visits be organised, eg will you get more and more detail or concentrate on getting the detail of separate sections?

- Will pupils be given specific instructions before each visit, eg to look at one particular area in detail?

> Use the prompt questions for less able pupils or for the first time the strategy is used.

(T) Pupils devise a creative strategy – a thinking skill.

(T) The review of strategies moves pupils towards more successful approaches to making sense of any source of data, ie big picture and attention to detail.

- Will the diagram be divided up at the beginning with each person having responsibility for a section?

Including a competitive element works really well. The pupils make sure that there is no cheating and that everyone gets an equitable length of time to look at the diagram. Remind them of the need to note down any changes to the strategy they use.

At the end of the allocated time pupils should summarise their strategies and display their posters. These are compared with the original. Pupils are invited to judge the poster that most closely resembles the original.

Plenary

Conduct a whole class review of the different strategies used. Pupils will need to use their notes and articulate the strategy they used. This is a challenging task for many. Make a summary of the most successful strategies at the end of the session. Some groups operate by having the first person mapping out the 'big picture' with others filling in the detail in subsequent visits. Others divide the drawing into sections with each pupil having responsibility for a part of the drawing. However, it is important that pupils appreciate the importance of 'getting the big picture'. As details are added, checks need to be made and the drawing refined. This technique can be replicated in any task.

Most of the drawings in this lesson had a good resemblance to the original. The part that pupils found most difficult was the throat and the interconnections between the nasal passages and the mouth. Most were unfamiliar with this part of the body drawn as a longitudinal section. Pupils were very keen to look at the 'official' diagram to check their version. It was clear that they had memorised the main elements of the diagram, by using discussions and reviews in the group to decide what information had already been 'got' and what needed to be 'got' next.

Follow-up

The drawings can be left on display until the topic has been completed. Pupils can then add annotated labels to show their understanding of the process of digestion and the functions of the organs.

The human digestive system

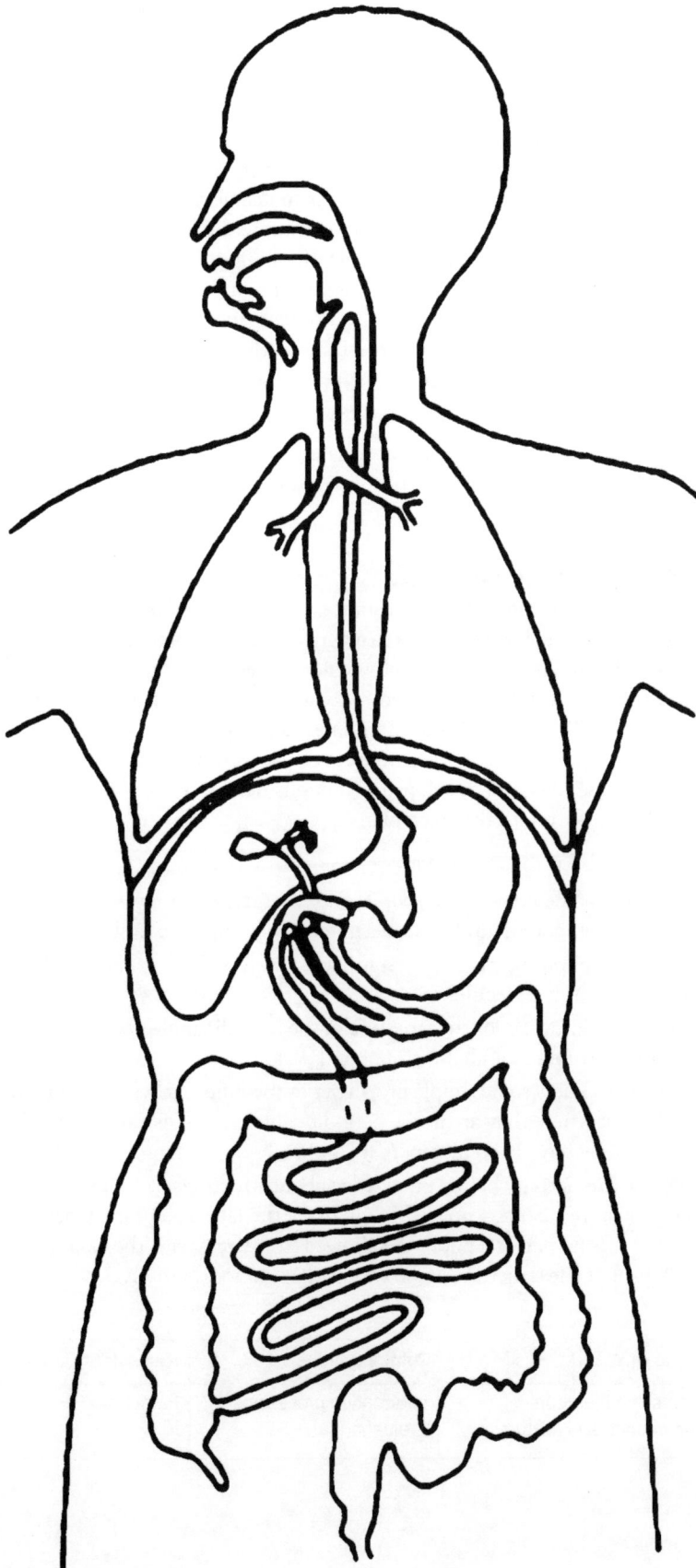

Outline

Considerable confusion surrounds the word particle. Clearly it has an everyday meaning as in particle of soot etc but it also has a more precise scientific meaning, both at atomic and sub-atomic level. It is not surprising that this whole area is subject to a number of misconceptions. In a similar way, atoms, molecules, symbols and formulae are often misrepresented in the media. To many people this area seems more confusing than a foreign language. Yet beneath this seeming complexity, application of a few simple rules can make the whole business straightforward.

This exemplar tackles some of these difficulties. Perhaps the difficulty in pupils' minds arises from the fact that the word molecule is used to describe the makeup of both elements and compounds and that it is the type of molecule that decides whether it is an element or a compound. There are two separate activities in this exemplar: the first activity is intended to develop pupils' thinking by looking at the cognitive conflicts set up by these issues; the second activity focuses on some other links and misconceptions which pupils have in the field of particles, symbols, formulae and the periodic table. The two exercises in this activity need not be carried out at the same time. The first could be carried out in Year 8 and the second in Year 9 if you wish. It is probably better to carry out activity 1 before activity 2.

In the first activity pupils have to interpret the imaginary contents of a box containing atoms and molecules. In the second, they have to choose the *'odd one out'* and give a reason for this in each case.

> The situation is further complicated by the fact that some elements exist as diatomic molecules, and some as larger molecular arrays. Details of giant molecular or metallic structures are best left alone at this stage.

Pupils' prior knowledge and skills

Pupils may have met the concept that substances are made up of particles at Key Stage 2 and some may even have developed this to a concept of atoms and molecules. They will have examined the difference between physical and chemical change, but it is unlikely that this will have been linked to elements, compounds and mixtures or that they will have more than a rudimentary idea of these substances and the link with their primary particles. They may have met the word mixture during activities to separate substances. At Key Stage 3 these ideas are developed and pupils need to have some background in these before they can attempt this exemplar.

> At this level (Y8), it is not intended that the difference between ionic and covalent is known and the word 'molecule' is used loosely to describe atoms that 'stick together' in some way. Some colleagues may feel that we are creating a misconception for later on by so doing!

Some prior knowledge is thus assumed:

- Ensure that, for the first activity, pupils understand the principles of the make-up of elements, compounds and mixtures in terms of atoms and molecules.
- For activity 2, pupils need to understand what symbols and formulae mean in terms of atoms and molecules.
- Pupils need to know about the structure of the periodic table, its breakdown into metals and non-metals and also groups and periods.
- Pupils need to know some simple properties of the different types of elements, depending on where they are in the periodic table, as well as basic trends. This would normally have been met in Year 7 or 8.
- Ideally, use this activity before knowledge about structures of organic molecules has been acquired. Some knowledge will make the later examples in activity 2 easier. But it is far better if pupils are allowed to struggle with the examples, not knowing about the structure, and try to work it out for themselves.

Links

QCA Scheme of Work	Thinking skills	Key scientific idea
Unit 8E Atoms and Elements Unit 8F Compounds and Mixtures	Information processing Evaluation	Particles

Lesson objectives
Thinking skills:
- sort and classify information
- analyse relationships
- evaluate information.

Science:
- know that elements contain atoms of one kind only
- know that the smallest particle of an element is an atom and that of a compound is a molecule
- know that the same compound always contains the same elements joined in the same whole number ratio of atoms
- know that a mixture can contain elements, compounds or both, in any proportion
- use symbols and formulae to show the type and number of atoms contained in the substance, and whether they are combined or not.

> (T) Remember that the main thrust of the exercise is to develop thinking skills. Choose at least one of these objectives.

Context
Activity 1 was carried out with both Year 7 and Year 8 classes. Year 7 groups and less able Year 8 groups found the activities more difficult. With middle-ability and more able Year 8 pupils, pupils understood what they needed to do and got on with the activity quickly. They reported that they enjoyed doing this. They had to think about things like the molecule being 'upside down' to see if it was the same or different.

Along the way, all parts of the jigsaw need not fit together. This particular exercise is a hypothetical one. It is about developing pupils' abilities to classify and evaluate information. Pupils work out the inherent differences between elements, compounds and mixtures – and between two compounds containing the same elements but which are, nevertheless, different. The process is deliberately difficult – to produce cognitive conflict and promote discussion in the groups. If the process were an easy one, with simple elements, compounds and mixtures, this would not be the case and would not develop pupils' thinking. Some such compounds do not actually exist! Can **you** think of a real example of *oxo* and *xox*?

> You should choose no more than one or two of the most appropriate science learning objectives if you wish to formatively assess pupils' progress in science during the lesson.

> (T) In the discussion pupils talk themselves into understanding.

Activity 2 was carried out with Year 8 and Year 9 groups. Where pupils' knowledge and understanding of formulae was not well developed, they found difficulty if some of the more complicated examples were used. For this reason, it worked better with more able Year 8 groups and Year 9 classes. It was found to be useful revision for the end of Key Stage 3 tests and was also especially effective with a Year 9 group when the exercise was carried out after the end of Key Stage 3 tests in the summer term. Here all 29 examples were used and pupils were seen to interact well to identify *odd ones out*. They came up with some interesting answers, including one group who came up with number 4 in example 24 because '*it is the only one that they use to make spatulas*'. (There must have been a budding chemist in there somewhere!)

Preparation
1 Ensure that you check your assumptions of the pupils' prior knowledge (see above).
2 On this basis, decide which, and how many examples to give to the groups. Normally, all groups in one class should be set the same examples and should work their way through these. Providing different examples to different groups of pupils makes their participation in the plenary less effective. If the class is a mixed ability class, then it may be worth considering forming ability groups and differentiating by the number of examples given – arranging them by difficulty, easiest first. This will allow the lower-achieving groups to join in, in the first part of the plenary and some may therefore extend their thinking skills.
3 Reproduce copies of the pupil sheet for each group of pupils. Or select some examples, or create your own.
4 The time allocated to both activities can vary. Once pupils understand the tasks, they can work on the examples for as long as they need, or as long as is available.

> Fewer examples makes the activity easier. You can also make examples easier by having fewer atoms in the molecules in both exercises.

Introduction

As pointed out earlier, it is probably better that pupils have carried out activity 1 before attempting activity 2.

1 All sessions should start with a clear description of the materials and what groups are required to do with these.

2 Unless pupils are very familiar with this way of working, try out a sample example with the class as a whole, to elicit what possibilities can be considered in order to reach a decision. With younger or less able groups, we used more than one starter example. But keep them simple. It is important too that you keep away from any discussion of conflicts that might arise from the main scenario. For example, in activity 1, don't ask 'is *oxo* different from *oox*?' Use the opportunity instead to explain the process.

3 Activity 1 explores the fact that elements are elements whether they exist as atoms or molecules, so long as the atoms are the same.

4 Explain that the *o* and *x* are not intended to be symbols. This caused confusion with some groups. They are intended to represent different kinds of atoms. A molecule of a compound is the same whether it is inverted or not, ie *oox* is the same as *xoo*, but *oxo* is different from *oox*.

5 Activity 2 uses discriminators that include knowledge of:
- compounds and elements
- atoms and molecules, and the numbers of atoms in molecules
- states of matter
- the periodic table
- naturally occurring versus man-made
- pH
- constituents of air
- reacting quantities
- empirical formulae (in terms of ratio of atoms in molecules)
- different structural formulae (in terms of visual clues)
- incorrect formulae.

Group work

Pupils should work in groups of three or four to sort, classify and evaluate the information and come to conclusions. You need to circulate among the groups, and listen in to identify the sort of issues arising from the pupils' discussion, and those that will usefully feed into the plenary.

It is especially important when observing group work in activity 2, that you identify *odd one out* selections which may be 'scientifically inaccurate', but which may illustrate points and move the discussion forward, to aid class understanding. For example, in line 1, pupils may choose carbon dioxide as the *odd one out* because the other two are carbon monoxide. Discussing this in the plenary may elicit the fact that Co for cobalt is a symbol and the second letter is a small one; it is not a compound; nor does it contain oxygen; and so on. The **reasons** for the group choices are more important than the choice itself. Challenge the thinking behind these reasons to move pupils forward, both in knowledge and in thinking.

(T) With practice, you will become better at gauging how much introduction is needed to avoid pupils becoming stuck because they don't know what to do.

It is essential that all pupils understand the task before being allowed to move on to the group work, otherwise time is spent with groups clarifying what the task is, rather than working on the activity.

(T) Particularly enterprising suggestions need to be identified for plenary discussion – making notes may help.

(T) Sort and classify information.

(T) Evaluate information.

Plenary

Choose groups to illustrate issues arising from the group discussions which you have noted during your class scan. Get the whole class to discuss these in an order which best feeds pupils' understanding of the issues involved. The most popular choices in activity 1 should be identified and discussed. Although the examples given to the pupils are organized in approximate order of difficulty, you may wish to use a different order in the plenary in order to concentrate on the differentiation between the same or different elements (C, D, E, I, L), followed by mixtures of compounds (A, F, G) and then mixtures of compounds and elements (B, H, J, K).

In the *odd one out* activity (activity 2), pupils need to explain and then discuss the different choices they have come up with, and the reasons for their choice. Allow others to challenge. Direct this in order to aid both whole class, as well as individual, thinking and understanding.

It is particularly important when teaching to develop pupils' thinking skills that you emphasize to the class that, in many cases, there need not always be a clear or 'correct' answer. For instance, in example 13: nitrogen could be the *odd one out* because it is used as liquid nitrogen to keep things cold; or chlorine could be the *odd one out* because it is not present to any appreciable degree in air; or argon could be the *odd one out* because it is not present as a diatomic molecule, and so on. The issue is not whether an answer is 'wrong' or 'correct'. It is the process that the pupil uses to come to his/her conclusion that is important. It is not the destination but the journey to the destination that matters.

Follow-up

It is possible for pupils to work on this at home, as long as they fully understand what needs to be done beforehand. But the interactive group aspect is then lost, unless you make sure that a good whole class plenary happens once back in class. There is cognitive conflict built in to the examples and, having worked on the issues by themselves, pupils will find that the class plenary further develops their thinking.

You can design some more difficult examples for the *odd one out* activity. For example, in Years 10 and 11, ions can be introduced and examples can include covalent and ionic substances. Or, different oxidation numbers could be used as discriminators at higher levels (upper KS4 and post-16) and a wider variety of properties can be used to extend the *odd one out* scenario.

Again practice with the plenary helps gauge which issues to discuss and in which order.

(T) Sort and classify information.

(T) Evaluate information.

(T) Analyse relationships.

(T) Reasons as to why choices are accepted or rejected by the class need to be understood (metacognition).

ACTIVITY 1   PUPIL SHEET
Elements, compounds and mixtures

1. Imagine each o is an atom of element o and each x is an atom of element x.

2. What does each box contain – element, compound, mixture - in terms of atoms and/or molecules, elements and/or compounds? How many of each? Give as much information as possible.

Example: This is a compound containing
5 molecules of compound oxxx

oxxx oxxx

oxxx oxxx

oxxx

A
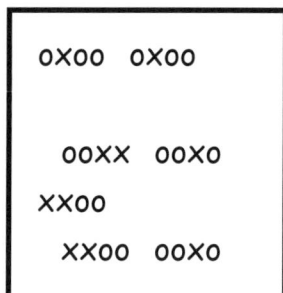

B
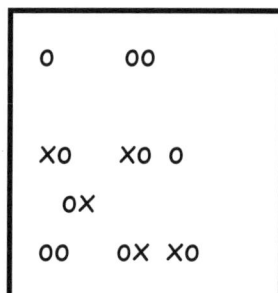

C
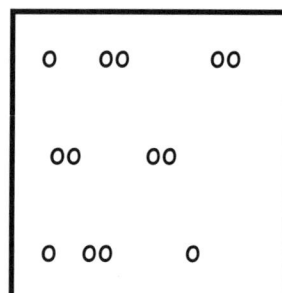

D
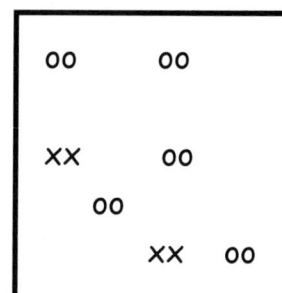

E
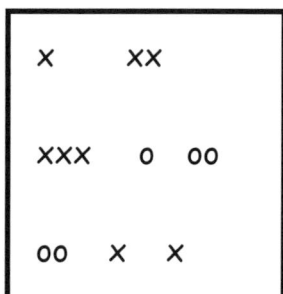

F
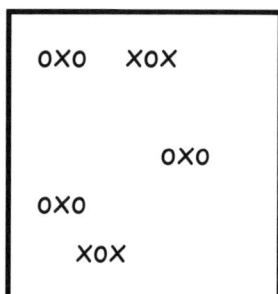

G
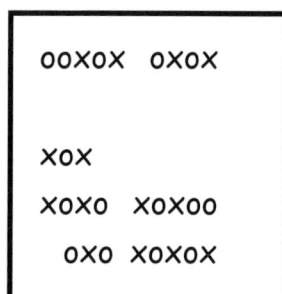

H
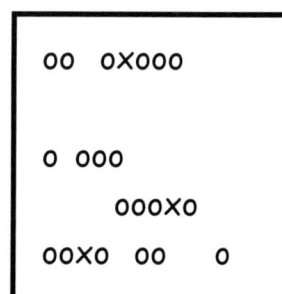

I
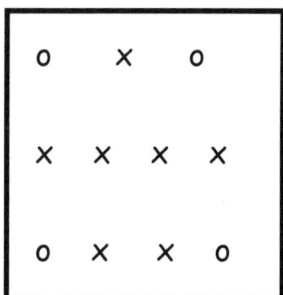

J
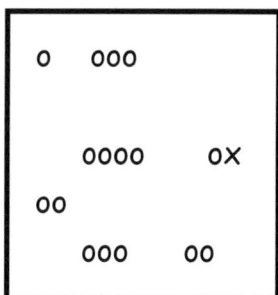

K
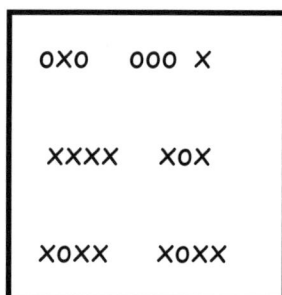

L
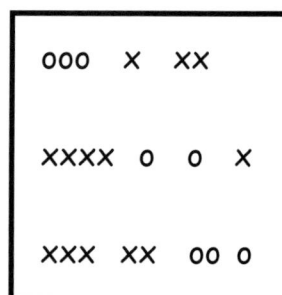

ACTIVITY 2

PUPIL SHEET

Odd one out

In each of the following examples, you have to choose the odd one out.

Say why you think the one you have chosen is the odd one out.

It is possible that some examples could have more than one different odd one out for different reasons – and still be acceptable. You may feel that one or two do not have an odd one out! However, try to find as many odd ones out in each example as you can! You can use any valid reason you can find: structure; numbers; even properties.

> Example H_2 5H   2H
>
> H_2 could be odd one out because it is the only molecule – or because it is the only stable form of hydrogen shown. However, 5H could be the odd one out because it does not contain 2 hydrogen atoms.

1.	CO_2	CO	Co	
2.	Co	CO_2	SO_2	
3	C	N	N_2	
4.	CuO	Cu_2O	$3CuO$	
5.	SO_2	SO_3	$4S$	
6.	$6H$	$3Cl_2$	$3HCl$	
7.	NO_2	N_2O_4	N_2	NO
8.	NaO	CaO	CuO	
9.	Na_2S	Na_2O	NaO_2	
10.	Ar	CO_2	CO	
11.	SO_2	SO_3	CO_2	
12.	$2SO_2$	$2SO_3$	$2O_2$	
13.	N_2	Ar	Cl_2	
14.	CaO	Na_2O	CuO	
15.	SO_2	H_2S	H_2O	HCl
16.	NH_3	N_2	H_2	
17.	He	Ar	Cl	
18.	CaO	Na_2O	K_2O	
19.	HCl	H_2SO_4	HNO_3	
20.	Na_2SO_3	$CuSO_4$	$3CO$	
21.	$5Cl_2$	$10Cl$	$8Cl$	
22.	I_2	Cl_2	Ar	
23.	NaO	CaO	MgO	
24.	Fe	Co	Al	Ni
25.	MgO	CO_2	Al_2O_3	$NaCl$
26.	$NaOH$	$Mg(OH)_2$	NH_3	HOH
27.	CH_4	C_2H_6	C_3H_8	$C_{10}H_{22}$
28.	CH_3COOH	$C_5H_{11}COOH$	C_2H_5OH	$C_5H_{10}O_2$
29.	$CH_3CH_2CH_2OH$	$CH_3CH_2OCH_3$	C_4H_9OH	

Outline

Energy is a new topic at Key Stage 3. For all pupils, however, the word energy will have been used in various contexts during their everyday lives, not always correctly. Many will be confused by energy *'forms'* and energy *'sources'*. They will use *force* and *power* incorrectly when they mean energy. This exemplar aims to clarify the terminology. The activity also reinforces the fact that, in practice, useful energy does have limits although, theoretically, the law of conservation of energy suggests that energy can be neither created nor destroyed, energy being transformed away to the surroundings, usually as sound, light and (mainly) heat.

Using *Energy* cards and *Process Shapes*, pupils are asked to devise a process that shows as many useful transformations as possible from one energy form to another. Different starting scenarios are suggested, by describing a situation and an input of energy. Using the *Energy* cards and *Process Shapes*, pupils produce a flowchart of process to process via energy transformations. This can then be affixed or copied on to their A4 sheet which outlines the initial scenario. Teachers may wish to set this as a challenge to different groups, so that a winning group can be selected at the end of the activity.

For example, *'a kettle of water is heated on a gas ring'*. Pupils are required to apply the new (transformed) form of energy to further use: *'the steam plays on a propeller'*. The resulting flowchart is referred back to the starting scenario.

> Visual processing and outcomes are very important in this activity.

Pupils' prior knowledge and skills

There is no reference to energy in the National Curriculum at Key Stage 2. Although reference will have been made to aspects of energy in plant and animal growth, during work on health and circulation and pulse rate in Sc2, and in heating and cooling materials in Sc3, no specific reference to energy in Sc4 is made. At Key Stage 3, therefore, the introduction to energy through energy resources and transfer will be the first specific reference to this topic. Before starting this activity, pupils need to be aware that energy can be manifested in various forms – and what some of these are. They need to be introduced to the principle of conservation of energy. It may be useful for pupils to experience energy transformations practically, either by demonstration or by first hand practical experience prior to carrying out the exemplar. This will ensure that they understand the context of the activity in terms of the different forms of energy and the processes of transformation involved, and can more easily visualise the scenarios.

Links

QCA Scheme of Work	Thinking skills	Key scientific idea
Unit 9I Energy and Electricity	Creative thinking	Energy

The Key Stage 3 Strategy Framework outlines *'Energy'* as a *'Key Idea'*. Here the idea of energy conservation is referred to in terms of energy *transfer* or *transformation*. Both terms are equally acceptable but you need to adopt a consistent approach. Energy *transfer* is used with reference to *transferring* energy from place to place. Energy *transformation* is used with reference to words such as *changed* or *converted*. In this exemplar we have used the latter term.

Lesson objectives

Thinking skills:

- generate and extend ideas
- apply imagination
- look for alternative innovative outcomes.

Science:

- realise that energy is not destroyed but changed from one form to another (law of conservation of energy)

- know that useful energy changes usually involve transformations from one form to another
- know that energy is usually eventually dissipated as heat into the surroundings (non-useful energy).

Context

This exemplar is intended to be an entertaining and challenging way for pupils to develop an understanding of the following issues and, in the process, develop their creative thinking skills through the use of imagination and innovation:

- the principle of conservation of energy is illustrated
- the different forms in which energy can express itself and be stored will be reinforced
- the transformation of energy from one form to another, with the associated losses of useful energy in the process through heat and sound will be discussed.

This exemplar was carried out with several Year 9 classes after they had experienced energy transformations practically.

Preparation

1 Photocopy the *Energy* cards and *Process Shapes*, cut them up and place them in envelopes. They may be laminated for longer life. More than one set of *Energy* cards may be needed for some scenarios.

2 Print each Scenario at the top of an A4 sized sheet of paper (or A3 which gives more space). This gives pupils space in which to display the process which they have developed.

Introduction

1 If pupils have not experienced energy transformations practically, you will need to explain the principle of conservation of energy and the fact that useful energy is changed, converted or transformed into other forms of energy. Pupils need to know that, eventually, energy is dissipated as heat or sound to the surroundings. An efficient process minimises these losses.

2 Carefully explain the task.

'From the given starting scenario, devise a process with as many energy transformations (as counted by the numbers of arrows used) as possible.

You must stop when reason suggests that the amount of useful energy left is not sufficient to be converted further and be measurable.

Although in many cases answers will not be tested, they have to be acceptable to the whole class who, along with the teacher, will be the final judges of the winner.'

3 Work through the example scenario provided (page 70). As well as confirming the task in pupils' minds in terms of the science involved, this will exemplify how to physically use the cards provided.

4 Divide pupils into groups and set them off on their own first task/scenario. We would suggest that it is prudent for all groups of pupils to work on the same scenario and, once the first is complete, to come together for a plenary. This will identify any problems or misunderstandings.

5 Once the plenary discussion on the initial task is complete, you may wish to get all groups to work on the same second scenario which you choose, or you might allow groups to choose their own. You can take this decision after the completion of the first scenario, as the feedback will have identified the different groups' ability to deal with the task. If you allow groups to work on different scenarios, it may be more difficult for you to monitor the progress of the thinking during the plenary, but it does allow differentiation of the task for more able pupils, who will be able to develop their creative thinking skills even further.

6 Pupils with ingenuity will devise processes where a great number of energy transformations take place before energy is dissipated.

7 The activities suggested here refer to energy transformations within one system, where the useful energy is slowly dissipated. Watch out for movements from the system under consideration to other systems during the process. 'System jumping' is

> Forms of energy provided on cards include solar, light, kinetic, nuclear, chemical, sound, potential, heat, and electrical.

> Starting scenarios sometimes include an external input of energy to start the process.

> If pupils work on different starting scenarios, it is difficult for the final plenary to address and develop the same issues and conflicts.

> (T) Generating and extending ideas.

> (T) Applying imagination.

> **T** You may, in fact, be happy to include 'system jumping' in your activity. This leads to a 'Heath-Robinson' or 'egg-race' type of activity which will equally well develop creative thinking skills.

> **T** Looking for alternative innovative outcomes.

> **T** Applying imagination.

> **T** Generating and extending ideas.

not allowed – unless agreed beforehand. For example, if light energy from the system hits a sensor in another system, which trips a relay and starts a process which is powered by some other source of energy, such as a battery, then the energy of this new system, ie electrical energy, is now being converted. Similarly, kinetic (movement) energy output from the system under consideration might release a ball, say, which has potential energy because of its position. This, too, is a new system.

8   The possible winner in a single system is liable to be one where there is constant inter-conversion of energy rather than one which converts energy to a great number of different types – for example, a pendulum, where there is constant change between potential and kinetic energy (losing small amounts as sound etc) until the pendulum stops. You may wish, therefore, to make the winner the person who uses the most different kinds of energy (different *Energy* cards) rather than the one with the most changes (ie arrows).

Group work

Pupils worked in groups of three or four. After the initial whole-class introduction with the example scenario, groups discussed the next given scenario and the possible realistic transformations that could be gained from using the output energy as inputs for further processes and energy transformations. Although the process was difficult for pupils to come to grips with, we found that the full introduction to the exemplar and the whole class sample task, minimised pupil misunderstanding of what to do. They were able to work on the given task without any interruption. You will need to carry out class scans in order to listen in, and identify the creative processes that pupils devise for subsequent transformations. These scans will identify processes that have the best chance of furthering the flow chart (and those which do not!).

Plenary

Discussion is liable to centre round good springboards for subsequent processes and transformations. For example, many groups felt that conversion to electrical energy meant that the next step was simplified because you can do so many things with electricity: heating; lighting; movement; etc. It was also seen to be controllable. Other forms of energy were less popular because they seemed less efficient and energy was lost in the process, eg heat and light. This in itself was a positive outcome in terms of scientific awareness! You need to identify processes which both do and do not provide good springboards in order to lead the class discussion effectively. Use the different groups of pupils, to identify and develop a whole-class understanding of the basic criteria for success. You must allow the pupils, however, to judge and agree where the 'end points' are for each flow diagram, where energy output is not sufficient to drive the next process. This may be the subject of heated discussion!

Follow-up

Projects. Pupils may wish to spend more time with their groups outside class time on projects to develop this idea.

Working system. A further extension would be to insist that groups must also be able to produce a working system of their flowchart. This would limit the number of stages, since dissipated energy is liable to be much greater than expected, and processes to carry out suggested transformations will not be efficient enough to secure a measurable output.

'System jumping'. Another alternative may be to extend the process outside the given system (ie, allow 'system jumping' as described in the *Introduction*) to produce a 'Heath-Robinson' type outcome.

Energy transformations: possible starting scenarios

TEACHER SHEET

1.	A mouse runs on a treadle wheel
2.	A reservoir dam gate is opened
3.	A candle burns
4.	Sun shines on a solar panel
5.	A match is put to a gunpowder mixture
6.	A switch is thrown in an electrical circuit containing a cell (battery)
7.	Wind blows on a propeller
8.	A person rides a bicycle
9.	A jet of gas issues from the ground in a volcanic region
10.	A mass is placed on a see-saw
11.	The engine of a car (or other device) with a full tank of petrol is started

Energy transformations: example system

TEACHER SHEET

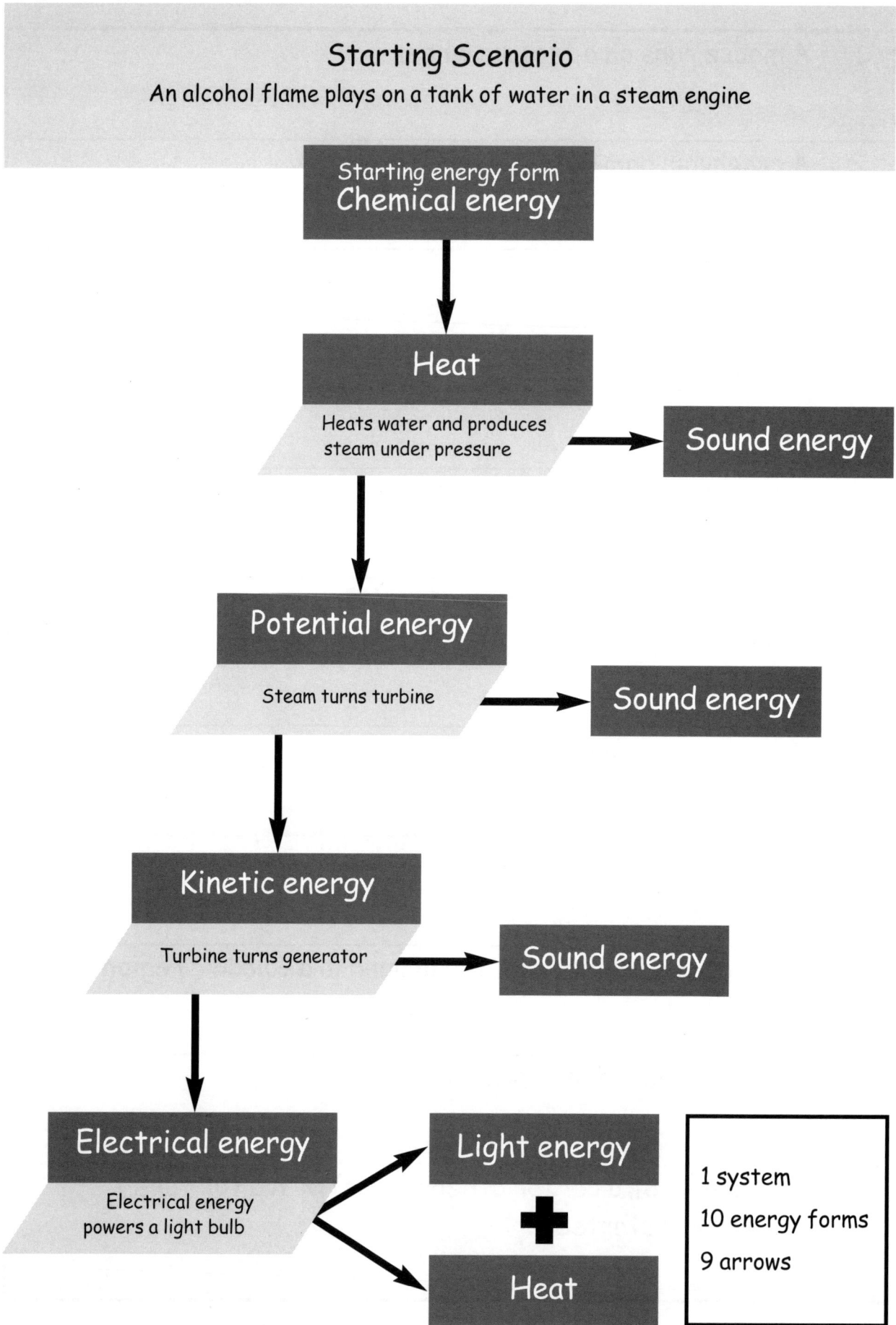

Starting Scenario
An alcohol flame plays on a tank of water in a steam engine

Starting energy form
Chemical energy

↓

Heat

Heats water and produces
steam under pressure → Sound energy

↓

Potential energy

Steam turns turbine → Sound energy

↓

Kinetic energy

Turbine turns generator → Sound energy

↓

Electrical energy

Electrical energy
powers a light bulb → Light energy

+

Heat

---

1 system

10 energy forms

9 arrows

Energy transformations

PUPIL SHEET

Starting scenario

Starting energy form

Process shapes: cutouts

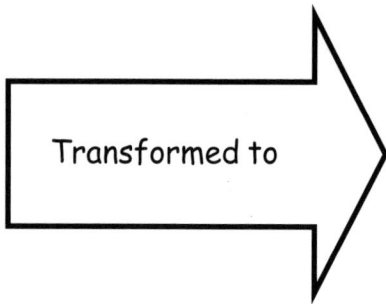 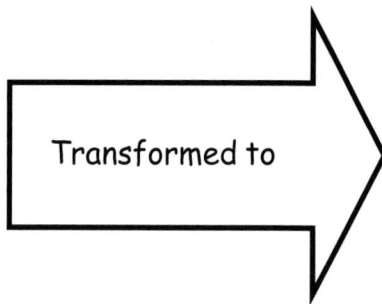 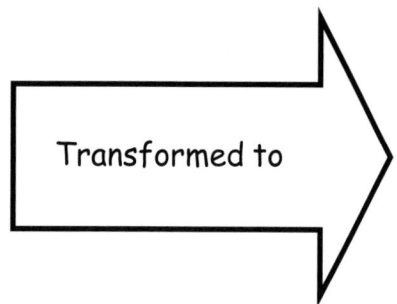

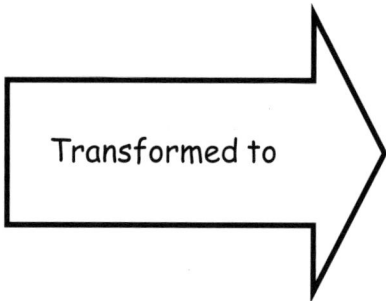 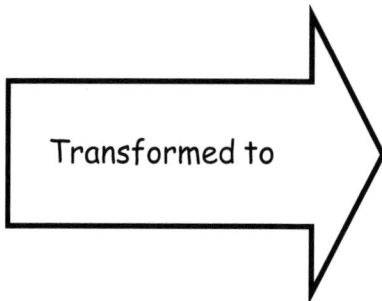 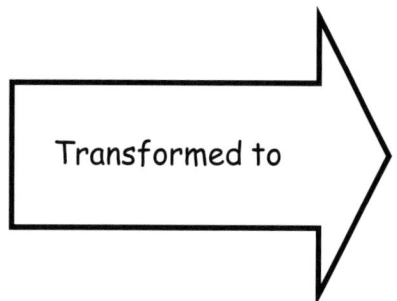

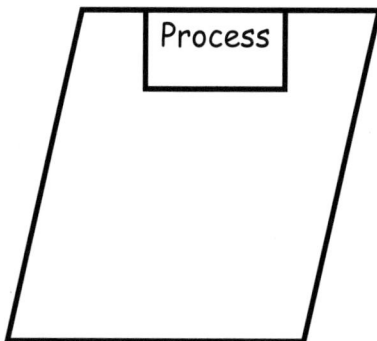 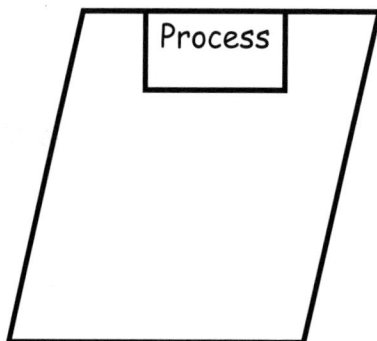 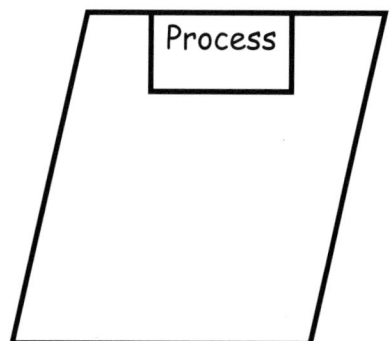

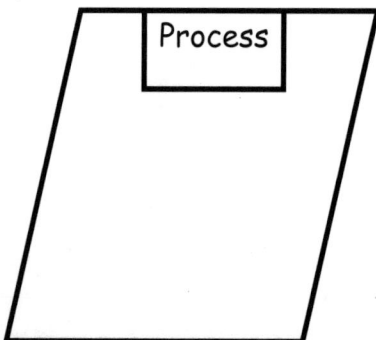 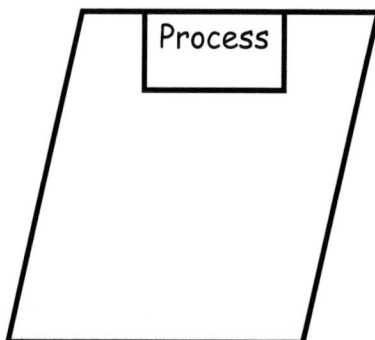 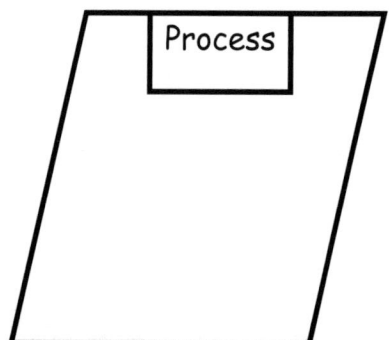

Energy cards

Potential energy	Solar energy
Potential energy	Solar energy
Kinetic energy	Light energy
Heat	Nuclear energy
Sound energy	Chemical energy
Electrical energy	Electrical energy
Kinetic energy	Light energy
Sound energy	Heat

Outline

Once pupils have carried out an experiment they are often reluctant to consider the outcomes further. Because accuracy and reliability of results can be one of the difficulties with their own experiments, an ability to evaluate and re-interpret is vital. Indeed, evaluation is a key part of modern science. How often have we heard or read in the media conflicting reports, for example *'science shows drinking red wine is good for you'*; *'science shows taking vitamin supplements is bad'*? The interpretation of the results of such studies depends on how the experiment was set up, how variables were controlled and how errors were considered. In this context an evaluation of the experiment in terms of accuracy, repeatability and reliability is very important. The purpose of this exemplar is to develop these skills. Pupils are provided with an account of a scientific investigation to evaluate. Pupils read the experimental account and answer questions using the data provided. The purpose is to get them to spot the good and bad features and to suggest ways in which the experiment or study might be improved. Pupils do not carry out the experiment. The focus of the activity is on selecting and comparing appropriate data to improve specific process skills for Sc1.

> Pupils do not carry out the experiment. One of the difficulties if they were to do so is to attach the 'ears' to get efficient heat conduction but that is another story. This exemplar concerns **evaluation** only.

Pupils' prior knowledge and skills

Pupils will have a sound understanding of fair tests but are likely to have had only limited experience of evaluation during Key Stage 2. During Key Stage 3 evaluation receives greater prominence in the scientific enquiry section of the programme of study. Before this exemplar is undertaken, it would be useful if pupils have explicit experience of discussing ideas of models, sufficiency, range and accuracy of readings as well as linking conclusions to science knowledge and understanding.

Links

QCA Scheme of Work	Thinking skills	Key scientific idea
Unit 8I Heating and Cooling Unit 8D Ecological Relationships	Evaluation	Interdependence (in this particular account)

Lesson objectives

Thinking skills:
- judge the value of the account
- develop criteria for judging the work
- have confidence in the judgements made.

Science (Sc1):
- consider anomalies in the data provided
- consider whether the evidence is sufficient to support the conclusions and interpretations made
- suggest improvements that could be made.

Context

This exemplar was mainly carried out with classes in Year 8, and it also worked well with a Year 10 class. With Year 8 classes, some pupils were concerned about the lack, as they saw it, of a control experiment. They were reminded that the focus of the work was on selecting and comparing data. Sometimes those who had weak mathematical skills found dealing with the data difficult.

Some pupils found the results confusing because two independent variables are being changed in the table: water volume and ear size. In these cases providing pupils with separate sets of data usually overcame this problem by obviating the need for pupils to select the correct sets of data for comparison. For example, separate tables, one for 100 cm³ volume, one for 250cm³ volume, one for 500 cm³ volume, and/or another set where the same ear sizes can be compared was found to help. These are produced on pages 77 - 79.

Preparation

1 You will need to judge whether your pupils will be able to select the correct data for comparison, even using the 'clues' given below the table. In case of difficulty, you may wish to give them separate sets of data.

2 Information sheets are provided in different formats (pages 77 - 79). Decide which ones to choose for which groups, depending on their prior attainment. Supply sufficient copies of these sheets – at least one between two.

3 Reproduce copies of the evaluation sheet for groups to complete – one per group of four. Alternatively, if access to ICT is available, the evaluation sheet could be provided as a *Word* document and pupils could fill it in on computers. The answer sections would then expand to fit the pupils' answers.

4 You may also need copies of whatever departmental guidance is used for pupils to judge their performance in scientific enquiry, eg 'pupil speak' versions of Sc1.

Introduction

1 Use a quick starter activity. For example, get pupils to quickly recall what evaluation of an investigation involves, or give them an example of experimental data to discuss, such as a graph with anomalous values.

2 Introduce the activity to the class and explain that they need to read the account of the investigation.

3 Divide the pupils into groups. Pupils can work in pairs to read the experimental account and then in groups of four to answer the questions, and complete the evaluation.

4 Provide a diagram of the apparatus if you think it will help.

5 Explain that they need to work in groups. They should answer the questions on the pupils' evaluation sheet in order to judge the quality of the report.

Depending on the experience of pupils, you may need to offer some guidance on what results to compare.

6 For lower attaining groups, you may need to provide separate sets of data. If these are shared between different groups then the activity takes less time. The plenary session will not be affected as all pupils will have had access to at least some of the same data.

7 Pupils need to be given instruction on how to complete the evaluation sheets (or in using the *Word* file). They must give reasons for their answers.

> (T) Assertion/reason questions are one way of getting pupils to follow through the logic of explanations.

Group work

Pupils worked in pairs to read the account and in groups of four to answer the questions on the evaluation sheet. In most cases this worked well and generated some good discussions. Some completed the evaluation sheet as hard copy, whilst others worked on the computers to do so.

Class scans will identify any pupils who are having difficulty in extracting the data. Where this is really preventing progress one of the simpler data sets can be provided.

In one lesson some highly attaining pupils raised the issue of the accuracy of the temperature measurements and possible errors. The temperatures taken suggest that they were measured to plus or minus $1^\circ C$.

Many of the questions posed do not have definite 'right' or 'wrong' answers. The idea is to get pupils to give an opinion supported by a reason.

Class scans (and reading the evaluation sheets) will feed you with information about issues to raise during the plenary. Carefully plan the order for the plenary session.

> Some pupils had some difficulties with the language in the questions. You may feel that you wish to simplify this in some cases BUT remember that science is about literacy and the precision of scientific language, too.

> (T) Judge the value of the account. Develop criteria for judging the work. Have confidence in the judgements made. All these processes strengthen Sc1.

Plenary

The information you gained by class scans during the group work should be used to manage this part of the lesson. Keeping to the order that you have planned, take feedback from each group to identify key points, ensuring that all groups are able to make a contribution. Groups should explain their strategies and the reasons for their decisions. A blank OHT to record a summary of answers to each question in turn is a useful way of collating group responses. Groups with similar or differing views should be encouraged to argue their case.

The key measure of managing an effective plenary is the amount of debate taking place, not the answers in themselves. In one of the classes considerable discussion took place about how good the model was. Generally it was felt it was good enough, but a number of pupils raised concerns about the 'ear' and 'body' contacts: were they all equally good? Other pupils raised concerns about how similar the starting temperatures were. With the most highly-attaining group of pupils this led to a debate about whether it mattered, ie how does the surrounding temperature affect the rate of cooling? Most felt measurements should be repeated – but how many times was a real issue. There was also debate about which reading(s) were erroneous.

Follow-up

Pupils could be offered the opportunity to set similar scenarios for one another or be given a similar activity from the AKSIS project (see *References*). The nature of the relationship could be explored further through drawing graphs.

References

Why Elephants Have Big Ears: Nature's Engines and the Order of Life,
Lavens, C., Gollancz 057506 722 5

AKSIS Investigations – Developing Understanding,
Goldsworthy, A., Watson, R. and Wood-Robinson, V., ASE(2000) 086357 310 X

Thinking Skills Through Science

Information sheet: version 1 PUPIL SHEET

Bethany and Joe carried out an investigation to model whether or not the size of elephants' ears affected their ability to stay cool or not. Their model consisted of a 'tin can' to represent the body of the elephant with aluminium foil attached to represent the ears. Their account of their work is given below.

In our work on variation and classification we became aware that some elephants had very large ears for their overall body size. As elephants live in hot climates we thought that this adaptation might help them keep cool. It was difficult to find enough nearby elephants to study, never mind the problems associated with measuring temperature change compared with ear size. Therefore we decided to carry out an experiment to model the real situation.

We took a variety of different sized containers (to represent the elephant's body) and attached aluminium foil 'ears' to each. We put hot water into each of the containers and measured the temperature of the water five minutes and twenty minutes after putting it in the can. The results are shown in the table below.

Volume of water in can (cm^3)	Size of ears (cm^2)	Temperature drop after 5 min ($°C$)	Temperature drop after 20 min ($°C$)
100	2	5	15
100	8	8	21
100	12	10	25
100	32	12	31
250	8	5	15
250	16	8	20
250	32	10	25
250	50	12	30
500	16	6	24
500	50	10	20
500	72	12	26
500	128	16	30

From our results you can see that the larger the ears, the greater the rate of heat loss for a given volume. You can also see that the greater the volume, the less heat is lost for the same ear size. Thus to lose similar amounts of heat bigger elephants need bigger ears. The reason for this is: the heat is carried by the blood from the body to the ears where a larger surface area results in greater heat loss. A similar but reverse system is used by birds who minimise heat loss in winter by standing on one leg.

Information sheet: version 2   PUPIL SHEET

Bethany and Joe carried out an investigation to model whether or not the size of elephants' ears affected their ability to stay cool or not. Their model consisted of a 'tin can' to represent the body of the elephant with aluminium foil attached to represent the ears. Their account of their work is given below.

In our work on variation and classification we became aware that some elephants had very large ears for their overall body size. As elephants live in hot climates we thought that this adaptation might help them keep cool. It was difficult to find enough nearby elephants to study, never mind the problems associated with measuring temperature change compared with ear size. Therefore we decided to carry out an experiment to model the real situation.

We took a variety of different sized containers (to represent the elephant's body) and attached aluminium foil 'ears' to each. We put hot water into each of the containers and measured the temperature of the water five minutes and twenty minutes after putting it in the can. The results are shown in the tables below.

Volume of water in can = 100 cm³

Size of ears (cm²)	Temperature drop after 5 min (°C)	Temperature drop after 20 min (°C)
2	5	15
8	8	21
12	10	25
32	12	31

Volume of water in can = 250 cm³

Size of ears (cm²)	Temperature drop after 5 min (°C)	Temperature drop after 20 min (°C)
8	5	15
16	8	20
32	10	25
50	12	30

Volume of water in can = 500 cm³

Size of ears (cm²)	Temperature drop after 5 min (°C)	Temperature drop after 20 min (°C)
16	6	24
50	10	20
72	12	26
128	16	30

From our results you can see that the larger the ears, the greater the rate of heat loss for a given volume. You can also see that the greater the volume the less heat is lost for the same ear size. Thus to lose similar amounts of heat bigger elephants need bigger ears. The reason for this is that the heat is carried by the blood from the body to the ears, where a larger surface area results in greater heat loss. A similar but reverse system is used by birds who minimise heat loss in winter by standing on one leg.

Information sheet: version 3 PUPIL SHEET

Bethany and Joe carried out an investigation to model whether or not the size of elephants' ears affected their ability to stay cool or not. Their model consisted of a 'tin can' to represent the body of the elephant with aluminium foil attached to represent the ears. Their account of their work is given below.

In our work on variation and classification we became aware that some elephants had very large ears for their overall body size. As elephants live in hot climates we thought that this adaptation might help them keep cool. It was difficult to find enough nearby elephants to study, never mind the problems associated with measuring temperature change compared with ear size. Therefore we decided to carry out an experiment to model the real situation.

We took a variety of different sized containers (to represent the elephant's body) and attached aluminium foil 'ears' to each. We put hot water into each of the containers and measured the temperature of the water five minutes and twenty minutes after putting it in the can. The results are shown in the table below.

Size of ears (cm²)	Volume of water in can (cm³)	Temperature drop after 5 min (°C)	Temperature drop after 20 min (°C)
2	100	5	15
8	100	8	21
8	250	5	15
12	100	10	25
16	250	8	20
16	500	6	24
32	100	12	31
32	250	10	25
50	250	12	30
50	500	10	20
72	500	12	26
128	500	16	30

From our results you can see that the larger the ears, the greater the rate of heat loss for a given volume. You can also see that the greater the volume, the less heat is lost for the same ear size. Thus to lose similar amounts of heat, bigger elephants need bigger ears. The reason for this is that the heat is carried by the blood from the body to the ears, where a larger surface area results in greater heat loss. A similar but reverse system is used by birds who minimise heat loss in winter by standing on one leg.

Evaluation

1. Could you repeat the experiment from the information provided?

Answer:
Reason:

2. Was the model experiment reasonable?

Answer:
Reason:

3. Was the test fair?

Answer:
Reason:

4. Were sufficient readings taken?

Answer:
Reason:

5. Was the range of readings taken sufficient?

Answer:
Reason:

Evaluation – continued

6. How accurate were the readings?

Answer:
Reason:

7. Were there any results in the table that you might particularly want to check and, if so, why?

Answer:
Reason:

8. Is the conclusion sound, based on the results?

Answer:
Reason:

9. Is a clear link made between the results and science knowledge and understanding?

Answer:
Reason:

10. Are there improvements you could suggest?

1.
2.
3.
4.

Outline

Pupils learn about floating and sinking from their early years. In Reception class they experiment with water and with many solids in water. Outside school, they will swim, perhaps fish, sail in boats or play with model boats. In the home and at play they gain a vast personal knowledge of things that float and other things that sink. Although they will have assimilated a lot of data about floating and sinking, they will not in many cases have evaluated this data to come to some opinion of why some things float and others sink. This is acquired knowledge, which is rarely articulated and tested.

This exemplar uses pupils' past experiences and asks them to investigate the issues that are important in deciding whether objects float or sink in liquids (usually water). In other words, pupils will evaluate the data, and try to come to terms with the conflicts that the data raises. There are three activities:

1　True or False?
2　The Sinking of the Titanic.
3　Why Do Things Float?

In each of these activities pupils are given statements about floating and/or sinking and asked to evaluate them. The first activity raises awareness of some misconceptions in floating and sinking. The second allows pupils to evaluate which are the most likely reasons why the Titanic sank. The third activity allows pupils to use their deductions to select the most important statements, order them logically and arrive at a theory for flotation.

> (T) Such knowledge may contain misconceptions and contradictions. This is critical in understanding the process of argument.

Pupils' prior knowledge and skills

At Key Stage 2 pupils will have experienced upthrust by weighing objects in air and then in water using a forcemeter, but they will probably not have done this with objects that float. This is addressed in this exemplar.

> The Activity also addresses pupils' literacy skills of summarising and collating as well as producing a piece of extended writing.

Links

QCA Scheme of Work	Thinking skills	Key scientific idea
Unit 7K Forces and Their Effects	Evaluation	Forces

Lesson objectives

Thinking skills:
- evaluating information
- judging the value of what is read
- developing confidence in judgments
- hypothesizing.

Science:
- know that when objects are immersed in water there is an upthrust on them
- know that when objects float the upthrust is equal to the weight of the object
- know that upthrust is different in different liquids
- draw conclusions from experimental results.

> (T) The main thinking objective is evaluation. The other objectives are sub-sets of this.

Context

This exemplar was carried out by several Year 7 classes. Most of them found the activities motivating and entertaining. Activity 1 led to a lot of group discussion (and even argument!) in the process of coming to group decisions about the statements. Similarly, activity 2 resulted in some interesting group discussion. For some groups, however, the amount of information provided proved to be difficult for them to deal with. In these cases, reducing the number of items to consider helped the concentration of some pupils. activity 3 proved stretching for some of the less able groups and those with literacy problems because it deals with the interpretation and ordering of text, as well as the ability to understand scientific concepts. Nevertheless, all pupils were able to do the activity. The more able groups selected more statements and included those which addressed the more difficult concepts. In the end, the paragraph which pupils produced

> All of the statements in Activity 3 are true. However, many of those in Activity 1 are not.

provided the basis of some interesting whole-class plenary discussions, entailing a fair amount of conflict and resulting in some good construction processes.

Preparation

1 Photocopy the sheets for each activity, either as a sheet of A4, on which pupils write, or cut up into cards. Pupils will use these to discuss the issues and make notes.
2 Assess the ability of pupils in your groups so that you can decide which sheet of statements, and how many to use in each activity.
3 The cards may be laminated for longer life.

Introduction

1 In a whole-class introduction, address the floating/sinking scenario by eliciting from pupils that some things float and some things sink in liquids. As a quick starter activity, you can read out a list of materials. Ask pupils to indicate (thumbs up or down – or horizontal if they don't know) whether the material will float or sink in water. This will also give you a useful indication of pupils' current understanding of what floats and what sinks.
2 The task in this exemplar is for pupils to find out reasons for floating or sinking by evaluating the statements they are given. Each of the three activities approaches this in a different way. Deal with one activity at a time. The three activities in sequence build up an increasing awareness of floating and sinking. If lesson time is short, you may wish to split the three activities to fit into two lessons rather than attempt them all in one go.
3 The preferred order is to start with activity 1: *True or False?* The pupils sort the statements into those that are 'true', 'false', and 'partly true'. They need to be able to explain why they have categorised the statement in a particular way.
4 Once pupils have taken activity 1 as far as you feel they can, you can carry out a class mini-plenary before moving on to the next activity *The Sinking of the Titanic*. In activity 2 groups can be given one, two or more statements to evaluate. Much depends on the time available and the ability of the pupils to discuss the scenarios. All groups should carry out the same task, however, to aid discussion in the plenary.
5 Activity 3 *Why Do Things Float?* enables pupils to develop an hypothesis about floating. Once they have reached a conclusion by discussing with each other, ordering the statements and combining them into a principle of flotation, each group should be able to explain to the class why they decided on the outcome that they did.

Group work

Group work is carried out for each of the activities in turn, with pupils working in groups of three or four. During this time you will carry out class scans to check for major differences between groups that can be used during each mini-plenary session. Note any interesting discussion points that can be used. As pupils move through the activities they will build up knowledge of floating and sinking and should be able to discuss the issues more deeply as they become more informed. For example, having completed activity 1, pupils were more aware of which aspects of floating and sinking were true, and were able to use this knowledge in their discussions on the sinking of the Titanic. They were able to discard some statements as obviously untrue. However, this newly gained knowledge also proved to cause problems in some cases. For example, knowing that steel sinks and polystyrene foam floats made statement 2 more appealing to some! So, knowledge gained in the earlier activities can feed cognitive conflict in the later ones!

Plenary

Manage the whole-class discussion in between activities using the observations you made during the group work. Take feedback from the different groups. Ask which is the most 'popular' reason – and why? What reasons do pupils give and what arguments are put forward to justify their choices? Once the discussion in the mini-plenary has been taken as far as it can, pupils should be set off on the next activity. You may wish to change the

The tasks can be made easier by (a) limiting the number of statements to which pupils have access in each section, and (b) selecting statements which are easier to evaluate – and leaving out the more difficult statements.

Cutting up the statements into cards makes for more 'active' participation by pupils, and helps some with the ordering of information.

You may wish to limit the discussions to water.

The reference to water pushing down as well as up in the last statement in Activity 2 is a distractor to link with pressure at a point in a liquid. This will, of course, only be a distractor if the pupils have covered this work, which is not normally addressed till Year 9.

Evaluating information.

Developing confidence in judgements.

Hypothesising.

The Titanic sank because it hit an iceberg and was holed. Ships float because the average overall density of metal, air and people is less than that of the water. Adding water (holing the ship) will upset this balance and the ship sinks lower in the water. Individual bits of the ship (that may break off) are usually more dense than water and sink.

makeup of groups in the light of the outcomes from the previous activity in order to ensure that discussions are as fruitful as possible. Once all the activities have been carried out, you may wish to follow up with a discussion of the overall outcomes. For example, a further discussion of the outcomes from activity 2 in the light of activity 3 may prove interesting!

Follow-up

Pupils can carry out their own simple investigations to check their predictions and evaluations if the equipment is available, eg various solids (some which float), displacement cans, thread, newtonmeters, measuring cylinders, simple balances, beakers, water, etc.

They can also use secondary resources to research *Archimedes' Principle* and the principle of flotation.

Activity 1: true or false?　　　　PUPIL SHEET

Discuss and decide whether the following statements are true, false or partially true?

	True? False? Part true?
Heavier objects sink further than light objects in the same liquid.	
Even quite heavy things can float if the conditions are right.	
Solids with big particles float.	
It is trapped air bubbles round the base of a solid that makes it float. If the bubbles escape, the solid sinks.	
Things only float in water, not in any other liquid.	
Metals sink, non-metals float.	
Only light objects like cork and wood float.	
Objects that are waterproof float.	
Needles can float on water.	

Activity 1: true or false?   PUPIL SHEET

Discuss and decide whether the following statements are true, false or partially true?

	True? False? Part true?
When objects sink below the water level, they usually go all the way to the bottom.	
Whether objects float in a liquid or not depends on the temperature of the liquid.	
Heating a liquid may cause an object floating in it to sink.	
All floaters float in any liquid.	
All bubbles float. This is because they are completely surrounded by soap. If you surround an object completely by a layer of soap, it too will float.	
Things that contain air float. If you hold your breath, you float. When you breathe out the air, you start to sink and have to start swimming.	
Floating is all about liquids and temperature. The solid you use doesn't matter. If the conditions are right – it will float. For example, iron floats on salt water (a boat) but sinks in tap water (a key).	
Adding salt to water makes things float better.	
It is surface tension that sometimes causes things to float. The liquid grips on to the object. If the grip is strong enough, the object floats.	

Activity 2: the sinking of the Titanic   PUPIL SHEET

Discuss each of the scenarios for why the Titanic may have sunk. Which are the most likely and why? Place the scenarios in order, with the most likely explanation first.

Rough things float and smooth things sink. The rougher the surface of a solid, the more the water can 'grip' on to it and the more likely it is to float. Cork is very 'holey' and the water can grip on to the sides of the cork well, so it floats. The Titanic was fairly rough when it was built. As it came close to ice in the icebergs, this made it smoother and so the water couldn't any longer hold on to the sides as well. This is why the Titanic sank.

Steel boats would not float unless shipbuilders placed sheets of foamed polystyrene between the plates. This is why the Titanic sank. When it crashed into the iceberg, the structure was damaged and the polystyrene sheets floated out one by one. It took a long while for this to happen and so it was quite some time before the ship completely sank.

A chap called Samuel Plimsoll showed people where to put a line on ships. This line, when correctly placed, showed at which point the ship would stop sinking. Sometimes the line was put in the wrong place and the ship sank deeper. The Titanic had no Plimsoll line and this was partially why it sank. Despite the fact that everyone thought it was unsinkable, they forgot the Plimsoll line!

Archimedes was a Greek philosopher who found out about floating. He sat in his bath and didn't float. When he put his toy plastic duck in, it did float. He shouted 'Eureka' realising that it was the plastic that made things float. After this, he made a lot of money selling floating plastic toys for children. His friend Aristotle used the principle in making boats and made a fortune as a shipping magnate. He built the Titanic, but didn't stick the plastic in firmly enough. When it hit the iceberg, some plastic escaped. This tilted the balance and is why the Titanic sank.

Activity 2: the sinking of the Titanic   PUPIL SHEET

Discuss each of the scenarios for why the Titanic may have sunk. Which are the most likely and why? Place the scenarios in order, with the most likely explanation first.

When the Titanic hit the iceberg, water got in and made the Titanic heavier. It started to float deeper in the water (and started to list because of where the water was). This is why the Titanic sank.

Things only float when there is no water inside them. Put water in them and things sink. When the Titanic hit the iceberg, water got in. This is why the Titanic sank.

The bigger and heavier an iceberg, the lower it floats in the water. As an iceberg melts, it floats higher in the water. This is why the Titanic sank – it hit an enormous iceberg that was almost level with the water – and nobody saw it!

When water got into the Titanic when it hit the iceberg, all the pushing up that the water had been doing from the outside now started pushing down also from the inside. This, and the great weight of metal, tipped the balance of floating and sinking. This is why the Titanic sank.

Activity 3: why do things float?   PUPIL SHEET

All the statements shown are true.

Evaluate this data by selecting ONLY THOSE that you think are the most IMPORTANT ones. Using these statements in the most logical order, build up a paragraph to explain why, in your opinion, certain things float. Devise a PRINCIPLE OF FLOTATION.

You can select as many or as few as you think are important.

Floating is about balancing the weight and the upthrust.
You lower a solid as far as it will go into a completely full container of liquid. If you catch all the liquid that overflows and measure its volume in a measuring cylinder, it is usually the same volume as the object itself. If this volume is less than that of the object, then the object is floating in the liquid.
The further objects in a liquid sink the greater the push upwards, until they are totally under the water.
The further down an object sinks in a liquid, the greater the weight of liquid that overflows. This happens until the object is totally under the water when the weight of liquid that has overflowed remains the same.
All solids push down on liquids when they are placed in a container of liquid. This is due to their weight.
All liquids push up on solids when a solid is placed in a container of liquid. This is called upthrust.
The heavier (more dense) the liquid, the more likely objects are to float in it.

Activity 3: why do things float?   PUPIL SHEET

All the statements shown are true.

Evaluate this data by selecting ONLY THOSE that you think are the most IMPORTANT ones. Using these statements in the most logical order, build up a paragraph to explain why, in your opinion, certain things float. Devise a PRINCIPLE OF FLOTATION.

You can select as many or as few as you think are important.

Whether an object floats or not in a liquid depends on what the liquid is. It is the 'push' upwards by liquids on solids that make some solids float.
You can feel this 'pushing up' when you swim.
If you measure the weight of liquid that overflows when you lower a solid into a completely full container then the weight is usually less than that of the object. If it is the same, then the object floats in the liquid.
Things get lighter as you lower them in water because of the water pushing up on them.
All objects that float always sink a bit in the liquid.
When a solid is placed in a liquid in a container, the liquid level in the container goes up.
If you weigh the amount of liquid that overflows when you lower an object into the liquid, then this weight is the same as the change in weight of the object compared to when it was not under the water at all.
If two footballs of the same size are floating in the same liquid, then the heavier one floats lower in the liquid.

Outline

Although many pupils can link organisms together in terms of what eats what, they often have problems predicting what will happen in a food web as a result of other circumstances. In this exemplar, pupils are provided with a diagram of a food web. They are given an *Event* card, and have to predict what will happen to the other organisms in the food web under the circumstances described on the card. This activity encourages the development of logical thought. In science it is important that pupils learn how to predict the probable consequences of certain actions or events.

Pupils' prior knowledge and skills

Pupils are taught about food chains in Key Stage 2 and the concept is developed further in Key Stage 3 when the chains are linked together to form webs. Before undertaking this exemplar, pupils will need to be familiar with the concept of food chains and webs, including what the arrows indicate and what direction they should be in. It will be helpful if they know what the organisms look like but this is not really necessary. It is the consequences of the *Event(s)* that they will work out, and they should be able to do this without detailed knowledge of the organisms. Some pupils, however, will find this a difficult idea, and will want to know about the organisms.

Links

QCA Scheme of Work	Thinking skills	Key scientific idea
Unit 7C Environment and Feeding Relationships	Reasoning	Interdependence

Lesson objectives

Thinking skills:

- make inferences and deductions
- explain their thinking.

Science:

- work out that factors influencing the number of organisms in one part of a food web can have an effect on other parts of the web
- know that all feeding relationships within a habitat are closely related.

Context

The lesson was carried out with a Year 7 top-ability class. They had been doing the QCA Scheme of Work unit on the Environment and Feeding Relationships and were nearing the end of the unit. In primary school they had all learned about food chains and understood the relationships between the organisms well, but some still had trouble drawing the arrows in the right direction.

The class had experienced two CASE lessons and were beginning to get used to working in groups and arriving at a group answer. There were still some though who were reluctant to feed back to the whole class during the plenary and some (mainly boys) whose first question when they came into the laboratory was *'Will we be using bunsens this lesson?'* and who were always disappointed when we weren't.

The lesson was an hour long although it could be lengthened or shortened easily. Some pupils were unfamiliar with some of the organisms in the food webs and this needs to be taken account of in the preparation. Most needed an explanation of microscopic plants and animals, which also provided a good opportunity to improve their knowledge of a range of organisms. Most pupils in this class coped with the vocabulary but the pond web was a challenge for a class of lower ability pupils.

Although this exemplar is designed to fit in with the Year 7 unit from the QCA Scheme of Work, it worked well with Year 9 pupils as part of their preparation for the end of year test, and could also be adapted for GCSE pupils.

Preparation

1 Organise pupils into groups. Threes are good, and friendship groups worked well. Pupils were confident enough to argue with their friends about the possible consequences of different circumstances.

2 Decide on which food web to use. For one class that had not experienced complex food webs before, a simplified version was used during the introduction to illustrate what they had to do. For example:

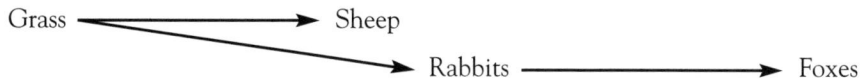

Grass ⟶ Sheep

Grass ⟶ Rabbits ⟶ Foxes

Explain that if all the sheep are killed there would be more grass for the rabbits. Their numbers will increase. There will then be more food for the foxes – and so on.

3 Decide from your knowledge of your pupils how best to organise the class.

4 Decide which *Event* card (or set of *Event* cards) will be given to each group. Which ones you use will depend on the ability of the group and the organisation of the class. Different groups can be given a different *Event* card for the same food web.

5 You will need to prepare the following resources:
- Select and photocopy one simplified food web for each group. Start with the woodland web if the pupils are unfamiliar with aquatic organisms.
- Copy the *Event* card(s) you have decided to use.
- Copy the prediction sheets – one for each group.
- Pupils may need pictures or other information about unfamiliar organisms.

Introduction

1 Pupils need to be tuned in. Start with the statement: *'Without plants we'd all die'*. Challenge pupils to think of something they've eaten that didn't come originally from a plant. You can even offer a prize if anyone can!

2 Another simple but effective starter activity is to draw a food chain on the board with a space where one of the organisms should be. Ask pupils to give an example of an organism that would fit in. Give them two or three different examples but keep it snappy – no more than five minutes. For example: given the food chain *'Grain – ??? – Owl'*, pupils wrote down the name of an organism that fitted in the space on a small white board and held it up. They then cleaned it off and the activity was repeated three or four times with different food chains:

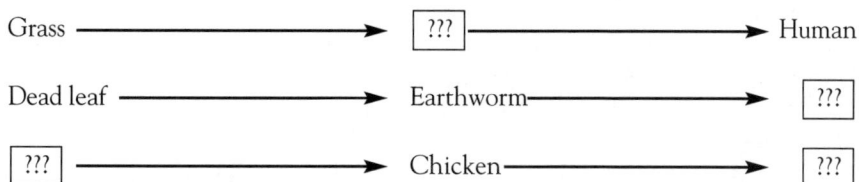

Grass ⟶ ??? ⟶ Human

Dead leaf ⟶ Earthworm ⟶ ???

??? ⟶ Chicken ⟶ ???

3 The introduction needs to be clear. Explain the task to the pupils. Make sure they understand what they have to do and how long they will have to do it. Explain that you do not expect them to ask you questions about how to carry out the activity once they have begun.

4 Decide, either from the starter activity or from your prior knowledge of the pupils, how much explanation about the food webs and the *Circumstance* or *Event* cards needs to be given. Some pupils were not familiar with the term 'population explosion' and many did not know what the different animals, particularly those in the pond food web look like or feed on.

5 Each group should be given a food web and an *Event* card (or cards) describing a particular circumstance. Tell them that they have to decide what would happen to the different organisms in the food web given the circumstance(s) described on the card(s). The group's decision should be recorded, with reasons, on the *Prediction* recording sheet. Tell pupils that they will be expected to report their

Use an illustrated food web. Cut out pictures of the animals and stick them on a web to help pupils visualise some of the less familiar organisms. Or you could use an interactive whiteboard.

(T) Be careful. It's easy to get diverted into looking at the different animals and plants and forget to get pupils thinking about the **consequences** of the different actions.

Laminating the circumstance cards can be cost effective if they are to be re-used.

It is useful to reproduce the food web diagram on A3 size paper or on an overhead transparency to use in the introduction.

Starter activities help pupils to become tuned in to the lesson.

This was a good opportunity to assess knowledge and understanding of food chains.

During the group work you do not want to be explaining again to each group what to do otherwise you won't be able to do a class scan.

group's findings to the rest of the class. A volunteer from each group can be selected to do this. Emphasise the importance of agreeing the outcomes and the need to explain the reasoning behind their decisions.

Group work

The class found the activity challenging and enjoyable once they got started and there were some quite heated discussions as to what the consequences would be if all the owls died. But many failed to see the consequences of an increased population of slugs, mice and shrews.

A class scan was conducted as the pupils worked. Notes were taken from overlooking and eavesdropping on the group work. These were used in the plenary. It is hard not to interfere. When pupils appeared to be stuck, asking open questions encouraged progress. If they looked as if they were not thinking the consequences through to the end, questions such as 'what would happen to...then?' were asked.

You will need to keep an eye on the pace of the lesson. It is better to pull the class together before they have all finished and to have a quality plenary than to wait for all pupils to complete all the cards and let some become bored.

Plenary

The information noted during the class scan is used to manage the plenary. All groups should be given the opportunity to contribute and areas of conflict should be used to promote discussion. Where a group did not follow the change in circumstance through to the ultimate conclusion, but merely identified an increase in population, the findings of another group who did follow through were used to provoke discussion. For instance, one group thought that if most of the small fish were eaten, then the pike would die because they had no food. They failed to recognise that pike had an alternative food source and that by eating more water boatmen some could survive. Another group had realised this and was brought into the discussion. The teacher notes taken during the class scan provided a record of the reasoning taking place in the groups and enabled this discussion to take account of the different group conclusions. Only one group followed the consequences in this chain back to the phytoplankton and none moved into other webs.

Pupils need to be given opportunities to justify the outcomes they have worked out. This is a crucial time when they explain their reasoning. Again the notes from the class scan can help you give all pupils the opportunity to explain something they found out – no matter how simple.

Most pupils enjoyed the task although some found it difficult to get started. They felt that by the end of the lesson they had not only learned how to work out the effects on populations of a change in circumstance, but also what some of these might be. Most also knew more about different organisms than they did before the lesson.

Follow-up

Pupils could be asked to draw a sketch graph of some of the changes in population they had been discussing. They could then bring their graphs to the next lesson, and some could be used as a starter activity.

You can make the lesson briefer or help less able pupils by giving each group one card only and then have a feedback. This worked well when the lesson was repeated with pupils who were not used to working in groups for extended tasks. More able pupils could cope with more than one card at a time.

(T) Reasoning skills. Pupils need to be able to explain their reasoning in relation to likely effects. This strengthens their ability to sustain an argument.

This reinforces numeracy skills.

Food Webs

WOODLAND

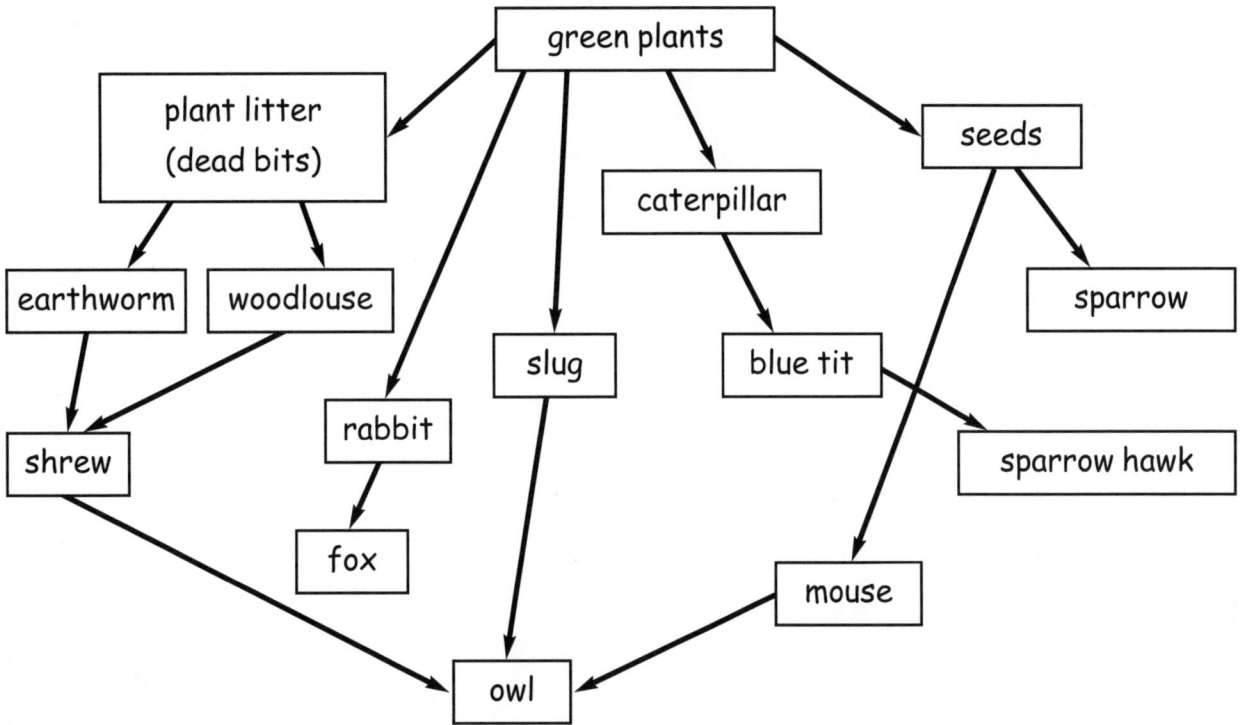

POND

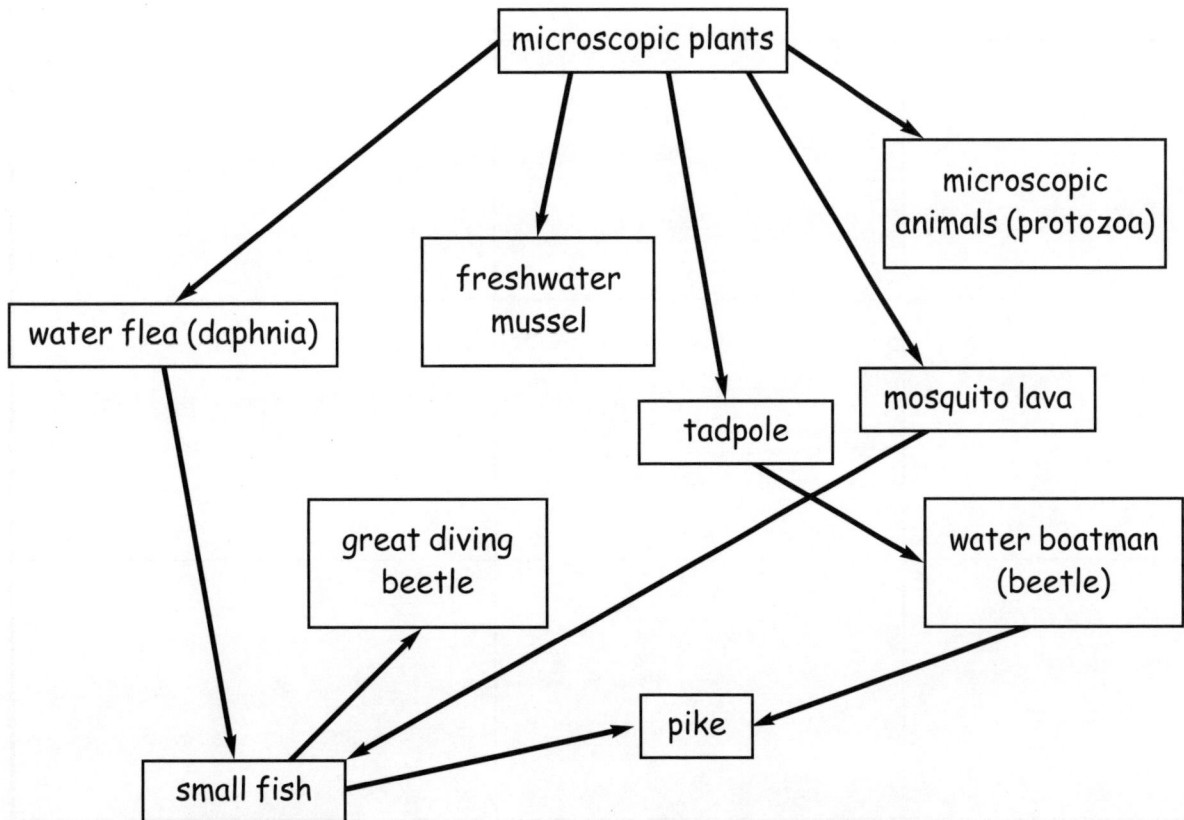

Predictions

Organism	What will happen to the numbers? Will they increase, decrease or stay the same?	Why?

Thinking Skills Through Science

Event or circumstance cards

PUPIL SHEET

WOODLAND	WOODLAND
No seeds are produced.	All the plant litter is cleared away.
WOODLAND	WOODLAND
The owls all die.	All the rabbits die from myxomatosis.
WOODLAND	WOODLAND
An insecticide is sprayed on the plants to kill insects. Which animals would accumulate the most insecticides in their bodies? Why?	The foxes are all killed.
WOODLAND	POND
There is a population explosion of caterpillars.	More pike are introduced into the pond.
POND	POND
A large number of frogs move from a nearby pond and lay lots of spawn that turns into tadpoles.	The pond becomes too cloudy for the microscopic plants to photosynthesise.
POND	
A heron eats most of the small fish.	

Outline

This exemplar is a simple sequencing activity. Challenge is provided by requiring pupils to work in groups, to agree the sequence and to give reasons. To arrive at a group consensus, and then articulate reasons can prove quite challenging for some pupils. The exemplar contains two activities which can be taught separately or linked. The first activity demands less of pupils, and was used successfully as a quick revision exercise at the end of the topic. With the less able pupils it enabled them to review their understanding in a non-threatening way whilst providing the opportunity for the teacher to assess their progress.

Different outcome options give flexibility. One class that was particularly motivated by the work they had been doing recently in English produced some interesting and imaginative poems. They also used computers to word-process the final versions. Another group of less able pupils produced a group poster, and achieved a similar outcome in terms of their thinking.

Activity 1: Sequencing. Pupils sequence the parts of the body through which a sperm will pass from the time it is produced to the point of fertilisation.

Activity 2: Creative writing. Pupils imagine they are a sperm cell and describe the journey they would take from the testis to fertilise an ovum. This can be in the form of prose (either written or using ICT), a poem or a poster and could be produced individually or as a group.

Pupils' prior knowledge and skills

Pupils will need to have been taught the process of fertilisation in human beings and the events that lead up to this (if you see what we mean).

Links

QCA Scheme of Work	Thinking skills	Key scientific idea
Unit 7B Reproduction	Sequencing Creative thinking	Cells

Lesson objectives

Thinking skills:

- sequence
- apply imagination.

Science:

- sequence the order of organs through which a sperm will travel to fertilise an ovum.

Context

In Key Stage 2 pupils learn about reproduction in terms of life cycles and there is no requirement in the National Curriculum to learn about the human reproductive system until Key Stage 3.

The lesson was carried out with two Year 7 classes. One was a lower-ability group and the other a middle band. Both classes had been taught the unit on Reproduction from the QCA Scheme of Work and this exemplar was used as part of the end of unit assessment. The middle band of pupils had been doing some creative writing in English and, after discussion with their English teacher we felt that it would be appropriate if they applied these skills to their science. They produced poems to describe the journey of a sperm and word-processed the final products. The lower-ability group produced a poster to describe the journey of a sperm. Some used the cards, stuck them on to a large sheet of paper as a scaffold, and annotated the diagram. Others drew an annotated picture.

Challenge and cognitive conflict are relative to the capability of the group.

This exemplar crystallises misconceptions and encourages better mental processing of the information.

The topic of reproduction can be challenging in terms of management, especially if there are significant numbers of immature pupils in the class. The nature of the class in this regard will determine the composition of the groups. In the lower-ability class, friendship groups would not have been appropriate and so the pupils were allocated to groups.

Preparation

Activity 1: Sequencing

1 Organise the pupils into groups. Allocating pupils to groups is advised with lower-ability or younger pupils. In the lower-ability group some pupils were very immature and if they had worked together it would have been difficult to keep them on task. These pupils were distributed among other groups where they could benefit from the more mature attitudes of other pupils.

2 Photocopy the cards and cut them out. Put them into sets – one for each group.

3 During the activity the cards can be moved about until pupils are happy with the positioning, then fixed to a large sheet of paper. Blu-tack can be used to keep the cards in place so that the finished poster can be displayed during the plenary.

Activity 2: Creative writing

1 Provide appropriate materials to each group according to whether pupils are writing prose or poetry, or drawing an annotated poster.

2 If the work is to be word-processed then pupils will need access to a computer per group.

Introduction

1 Set the scene by explaining why it is important to sequence. An interesting example is to think about the actions we take from the time we get up until the time we leave the house on a wet winter morning. If you think of the following actions: taking off your nightwear; having a shower; putting on your underwear; putting on your outerwear; putting your coat on; leaving the house; you can consider what would be the consequences if any of these occurred in a different order from that given! Some interesting images spring to mind.

2 Introduce activity 1 and explain to the pupils that they are to put the cards in the correct order showing the sequence of the organs through which a sperm cell will pass from the testis to the ovum. They are to work as a group and agree the correct order. They must note their reasons and be able to explain them to the rest of the class.

3 One of the cards (ovary) is there as a deliberate distracter. Pupils often mistakenly believe that fertilisation takes place in the ovary. This distracter card provides the opportunity to find out if this is the case, and for reasoned argument to occur between pupils who disagree.

4 Make it clear to pupils that they will be expected to explain their final sequence and the strategy they used to arrive at the final order. It is important that pupils are prepared to explain the strategy they used to work out their solution. They do not find this easy at first and may need some support in ordering their thoughts.

> Appoint a scribe who will feedback.

5 For more able pupils the sequencing activity is less of a challenge. For these pupils, the length of the activity should be kept short and the focus of the activity should be on the reasoning and strategy they use.

6 Many of the cards contain both the common term and the scientific one, eg womb/uterus. It is important that pupils learn as early as possible the correct scientific terminology and learn to use it in the correct context.

7 For the creative writing activity, you should stress that the application of imagination is one of the important aspects of the task. They should describe from a first hand perspective what the experience would be like, whilst retaining accurate use of scientific terminology.

8 Explain what the expected outcome will be, and the practical details, whether a poster, a word-processed document or other outcome.

Group work
Activity 1: Sequencing
Pupils should work as groups agreeing the sequence of organs through which the sperm will pass. Most groups in the more able class produced a sequence that was correct, although a couple of groups were determined to include ovary despite being told that not all the cards had to be used. This information was used to good effect during the plenary.

Plenary
Activity 1: Sequencing.

Able to sequence.

The outcomes of the group work were reviewed. Pupils were encouraged to describe the sequence of organs they had chosen and what their reasons for the sequence were. A group of pupils that had included 'ovary' was chosen to begin, followed by a second group which had the correct sequence and had not included 'ovary'. The discussion was then

A nice example of rhetorical argument succeeding.

broadened to include the whole class, using the information gained during the class scan of the group work to structure the progress of the discussion. Eventually, the groups that had not included 'ovary' convinced the others that they were wrong. A group that had decided that fertilisation took place in the uterus was then asked to feedback, followed by other groups that had correctly identified the oviduct as the point of fertilisation.

This is a good example of knowledge being shared in exploratory talk.

After the class had agreed the final sequence, a whole class discussion followed. Pupils used their knowledge of the process of fertilisation and subsequent implantation to describe the process they had gone through to decide the order of the organs, how they went about the task, and what strategies they used. This process enabled pupils who had not arrived at the correct sequence to achieve success, as there was no right or wrong answer to this part of the lesson.

Activity 2: Creative writing

Apply imagination.

Pupils could share their writing by reading some examples to the rest of the class. Some pupils may be reticent to read their own work, so this could be done for them. Or, pupils' poems could be displayed in the laboratory. Using computers to word-process the piece of writing was particularly motivating for the boys in the group who were usually reluctant to complete extended pieces of writing.

One particularly successful aspect of this activity was the way some pupils developed their imaginative skills enough to describe the relative sizes of organs and cells.

Parts of the reproductive system
PUPIL SHEET

testis	sperm duct
urethra	penis
vagina	cervix
uterus/womb	fallopian tube/oviduct
ovum/egg	ovary

This exemplar could usefully follow on from a science lesson in which pupils have extracted data from a variety of sources and are now ready to investigate relationships within the data – important science processes.

Outline

The skills of ordering, interpretation and manipulation of data are important for pupils to acquire, both in general and specifically in science. Such skills enable pupils to seek patterns and provide explanations when using reliable secondary data, rather than their own results. There are a number of parts of the science curriculum where it is difficult to make first hand measurements and the use of secondary sources enables these curriculum areas to be studied effectively. We are all exposed to claims which are based on large amounts of data that have been manipulated in a variety of ways. Frequently, axes are unlabelled, different (mixed) scales are used, or data has been compressed in a particular way to better demonstrate correlation. Pupils need to be aware of these issues, and need the skills to unravel and interpret such data.

In this exemplar, pupils are provided with a range of secondary data from which they are required to obtain information about the planets. They will interrogate this data to identify and investigate relationships. This can be done in three different ways:

- pupils extract and order data, draw a graph then suggest and explain relationships
- pupils use pre-ordered data to draw a graph, suggest and explain relationships
- pupils decide on relationships and explain them from graphs.

A powerful way of manipulating and analysing data, which can be used in this exemplar, is through the use of spreadsheets. This has the added advantage of linking to and developing pupils' ICT skills – and enables them to focus on the science and the thinking skills rather than the details of graph construction.

Pupils' prior knowledge and skills

In Key Stage 2, pupils are taught that the Sun, Earth and Moon are approximately spherical, and about periodic changes relating to the spin of the Earth and the movement of the Sun and the Moon. In Key Stage 3 this area of study is extended to the solar system, including the relative position and movements of the planets.

Links

Possible ICT link.

QCA Scheme of Work	Thinking skills	Key scientific idea
Unit 7L The Solar System and Beyond	Information processing Reasoning	Forces

Lesson objectives

Thinking skills:

- extract relevant data from secondary sources
- order data to find relationships
- derive relationships between variables.

Science:

- know the relative position of the planets
- use secondary sources to collect information about planets
- identify and explain relationships.

Context

Although the information about the solar system is readily available from a variety of sources, pupils can find it quite challenging to extract relevant data and identify associated relationships. The lesson was carried out with a Year 7 high-attaining class. They had just finished work on the QCA Scheme of Work unit The Solar System and Beyond. After the introduction, pupils were uncertain what to do when confronted with Data sheet 1. The teacher explained that it may be useful to compare the situation with a rail timetable: you have lots of information in a rail timetable but you may only want a small amount, eg the departure and arrival times of one train. Similarly with this data sheet you need to extract relevant data. He then set the following scenario:

You asked me 'Have you any information on planets?' I said 'Yes, here you are but you were not specific enough. You will have to sort out what you want yourself from all this data.'

At this point the lesson simply took off at a rapid pace with assorted graphs etc being produced, and lots of discussion and thinking.

The lesson took 50 minutes but could have easily been extended to 150 minutes. Some pupils had difficulty with the data sheets and care is needed to tailor the amount of information to the pupils' abilities. Similarly, some found graph construction challenging, for example the choice of appropriate scales.

Although this Activity is designed to fit in with the Year 7 unit from the QCA Scheme of Work, it also worked well with a mixed-ability Year 8 group and with highly attaining Year 9 groups. Middle- and lower-attaining Year 9 groups encountered some difficulties with the graph work. However, the use of pre-prepared graphs or ICT to draw graphs in these cases improved pupils' performance.

> ICT can help here and keep the focus on the relationship rather than graph construction.

Preparation

1 It is important to ensure that the focus of this activity is on finding and rationalising relationships by examining a range of data from secondary sources and looking for patterns and relationships. Make sure that you minimise any problems with data extraction and manipulation. Take into account the following:
   - pupils' familiarity with spreadsheets and graphing programs
   - pupils' ability to extract relevant information from sources
   - pupils' graphical skill levels
   - pupils' prior attainment (in order to ensure that the volume and complexity of data are appropriate).

2 Adjust the level of task difficulty by considering and selecting:
   - the range of information provided
   - the detail provided
   - the type of pattern or relationship to be explored.

3 Examples of data, from which appropriate information can be selected, are found on the Excel spreadsheet. Many other graphs are possible. Decide which to use.

> A variety of secondary sources such as texts, reference books, CDRoms, Internet access etc can be provided.

4 If ICT is being used to draw graphs, ensure that pupils can use any graphing programs appropriately. If graphs are being drawn by hand you may need to provide graph paper with pre-printed scales. This will enable some pupils to focus on the relationships rather than on the production of a graph.

5 Depending on the decisions you make, you may need to:
   - copy the data sheets from the spreadsheet, or use those provided as photocopiable masters
   - copy the spreadsheet to the network (if you have one)
   - provide graph paper
   - provide graph paper with pre-prepared scales
   - have a variety of secondary sources available
   - have access to computers with suitable software.

> For examples see AKSIS *Getting to Grips with Graphs.*

6 Given the large amount of data that can be made available, you will need to be careful about matching desired outcomes with time available. If in doubt adopt a minimalist approach – certainly for the first time. For example, pupils could be provided with the table and the graph from Data sheet 3a or 3b listing the planets, their distance from the Sun, and their orbital period and asked to identify any relationship and the reasons for this. See the options available in the *Introduction.*

> Keep it simple.

Introduction

1 Pupils need to be tuned in to the activity in terms of their knowledge and understanding of the solar system with a succinct starter activity. In the lesson that followed on from the unit: The Solar System and Beyond, pupils needed only to be keyed in on ways of extracting data. But you may need a more focused starter activity depending on the pupils' level of knowledge. Any such starter activity needs to be brief and to the point. For example pupils could be asked specific questions about the solar system, or could play a loop card game.

2 Decide on how to adjust the degree of difficulty as outlined above. Three options are suggested below to cater for different levels of attainment or time available.

3 Put pupils in groups of three or four to facilitate the rate of working and to provide opportunities for discussion and debate.

4 Introduce the task to pupils either using paper or ICT. Thus they are given either Data sheet 1 or the spreadsheet on their computer.

> (T) Care is needed to ensure that any use of ICT does not obscure the principal purpose of the lesson, ie the extraction of relevant data and the recognition of relationships.

Option 1

Pupils are given the task of extracting data from the secondary source (the Data sheet or the spreadsheet). They must order the data so that they can identify relationships. Pupils are told that the main task is to choose any two variables or properties, draw a graph (using ICT or otherwise), and agree what the relationship is between the two. They must be encouraged to give a reason for their answer (for instance: year length increases with distance from sun – further to travel, gravity force increases with increasing mass).

Option 2

Give pupils a spreadsheet (or table) containing information which is already ordered. Ask them to draw a graph, suggest the relationship in words and try to explain it.

Option 3

If time is short, provide pupils with graphs. Ask them to identify and explain any relationship. You may wish to give pupils graphs with the points plotted but no line, or graphs with both points and the line of best fit already drawn. Samples of these are given as Data sheets 2-5.

Group work

The class found the activity quite demanding but enjoyable. Once they were over the initial hurdle of extracting the data, the groups produced some good graphs and focused on looking for relationships. Some pupils found the idea of 'no obvious relationship' (eg gravity force v number of moons) difficult to grasp: *'if we have been asked to do it there must be a relationship!'*

> Extract relevant data from secondary sources.

During the class scans, it may become obvious that some groups are getting bogged down in data extraction while others may be having difficulties with graph construction. At this point you may find that intervention is necessary to ensure that all groups have something for the plenary session. Thus some could be given simplified data sheets and others could have graphs with pre-drawn scales on them. You need to ensure that by the end of the group work all groups have some information on possible relationships and supporting reasons to take forward to the plenary session.

> (T) Order data to find relationships.

Plenary

Use your observations from the class scans to decide which group to take feedback from first. In order to ensure that all groups have their contributions listened to and valued, it is important that the groups that have least to contribute are taken first. Take others in order, ending up with the group that has the best understanding of its findings. There may well be disagreements! For example, some lively discussion took place about whether there was a straight line or smooth curve relationship between a planet's distance from the Sun and its orbital period. This in turn led to recognition of the need to construct graphs accurately and the idea of 'best-fit' lines. Some pupils had difficulty accepting that an appropriate answer may be that there is no relationship, for example, between the gravity force and the number of moons. This in turn led to further debate about information changes over time, the completeness of evidence and other variables that might not have been considered previously. You may also find it useful to record key

> (T) Derive relationships between variables.

relationships in pupils' recent work on the solar system.

Follow-up

A number of pupils may need little encouragement to look for further relationships. These can be expressed both in general and mathematical terms either by using those properties listed, or by adding new ones. Websites, too, provide a rich area for both data acquisition and common misconceptions.

References

- *AKSIS Investigations. Getting to grips with graphs*, Goldsworthy, A., King, R. & Wood-Robinson V., ASE (2000) 086 357 3029.
- *Spreadsheets in Science*, Flavell & Tebbutt, John Murray (1995) 07195 71375.
- *The Planets*, McNab & Younger, BBC Books 0563 38469 7.
- Websites including *www.rogerfrost.com*

This can reinforce numeracy and/or ICT skills.

PUPIL SHEET

Data sheet 1: Table 1

Planet	Surface temp. degrees C	Day length hours	Year length Years	Mass cf Earth	Gravity force cf Earth	Number of moons	Diameter km	Distance from Sun millions of km
Earth	22	24	1	1	1	1	12756	149.6
Jupiter	-150	10	11.9	318	2.64	16	142980	778.3
Mars	23	24.6	1.88	0.11	0.38	2	6786	227.9
Mercury	350	1416	0.24	0.055	0.38	0	4878	57.9
Neptune	-220	16.1	165	17	1.21	8	49530	4496.6
Pluto	-230	153.6	248	0.002	0.06	1	2280	5900
Saturn	-180	10.6	29.5	95	1.16	18	120540	1427
Uranus	-210	17.2	84	15	1.11	15	51120	2869.6
Venus	480	5832	0.62	0.81	0.9	0	12103	108.2

PUPIL SHEET

Data sheet 1: Table 2

Planet Name	Type (rocky, gas etc)	Atmosphere (main gases)
Earth	rocky	nitrogen, oxygen
Jupiter	gas	hydrogen, helium
Mars	rocky	carbon dioxide, argon
Mercury	rocky	none
Neptune	gas	hydrogen, helium, methane
Pluto	rocky	nitrogen
Saturn	gas	hydrogen, helium
Uranus	gas	hydrogen, helium, methane
Venus	rocky	carbon dioxide

Data sheet 2

PUPIL SHEET

Comparison of planet mass with its gravity force

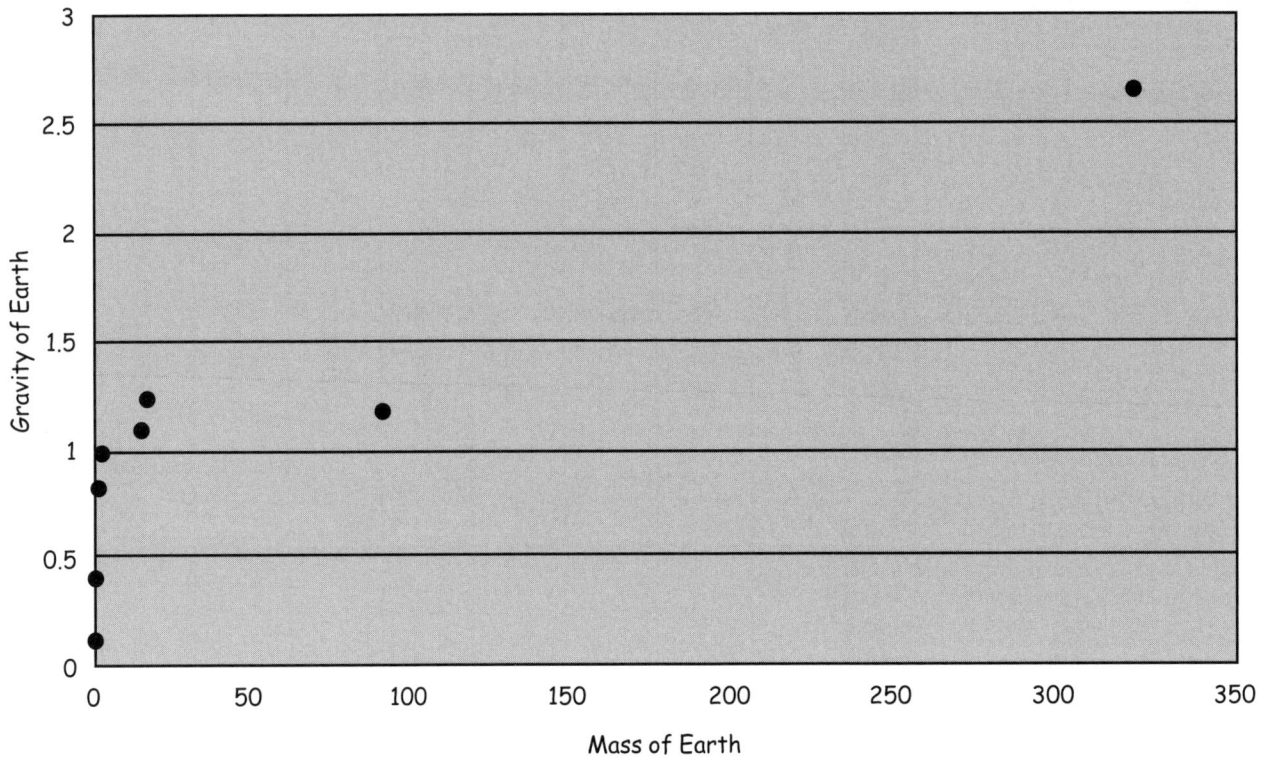

Planet	Planet mass compared with Earth	Gravity force compared with Earth
Earth	1	1
Jupiter	318	2.64
Mars	0.11	0.38
Mercury	0.055	0.38
Neptune	17	1.21
Pluto	0.002	0.06
Saturn	95	1.16
Uranus	15	1.11
Venus	0.81	0.9

Data sheet 3a

PUPIL SHEET

Comparison of orbital period with distance from the Sun (A)

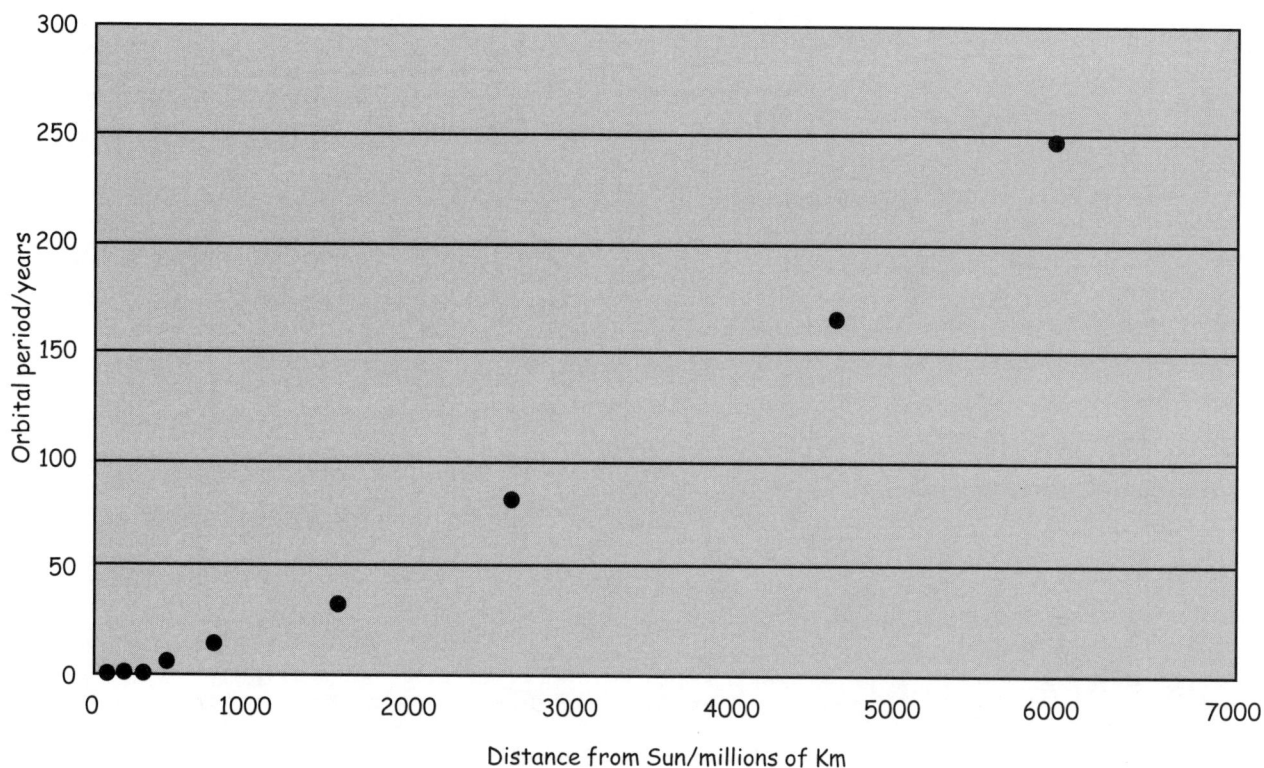

Planet	Distance from Sun millions of km	Orbital period (year length) years
Earth	149.6	1
Jupiter	778.3	11.9
Mars	227.9	1.88
Mercury	57.9	0.24
Neptune	4496.6	165
Pluto	5900	248
Saturn	1427	29.5
Uranus	2869.6	84
Venus	108.2	0.62

Data sheet 3b

PUPIL SHEET

Comparison of orbital period with distance from the Sun (B)

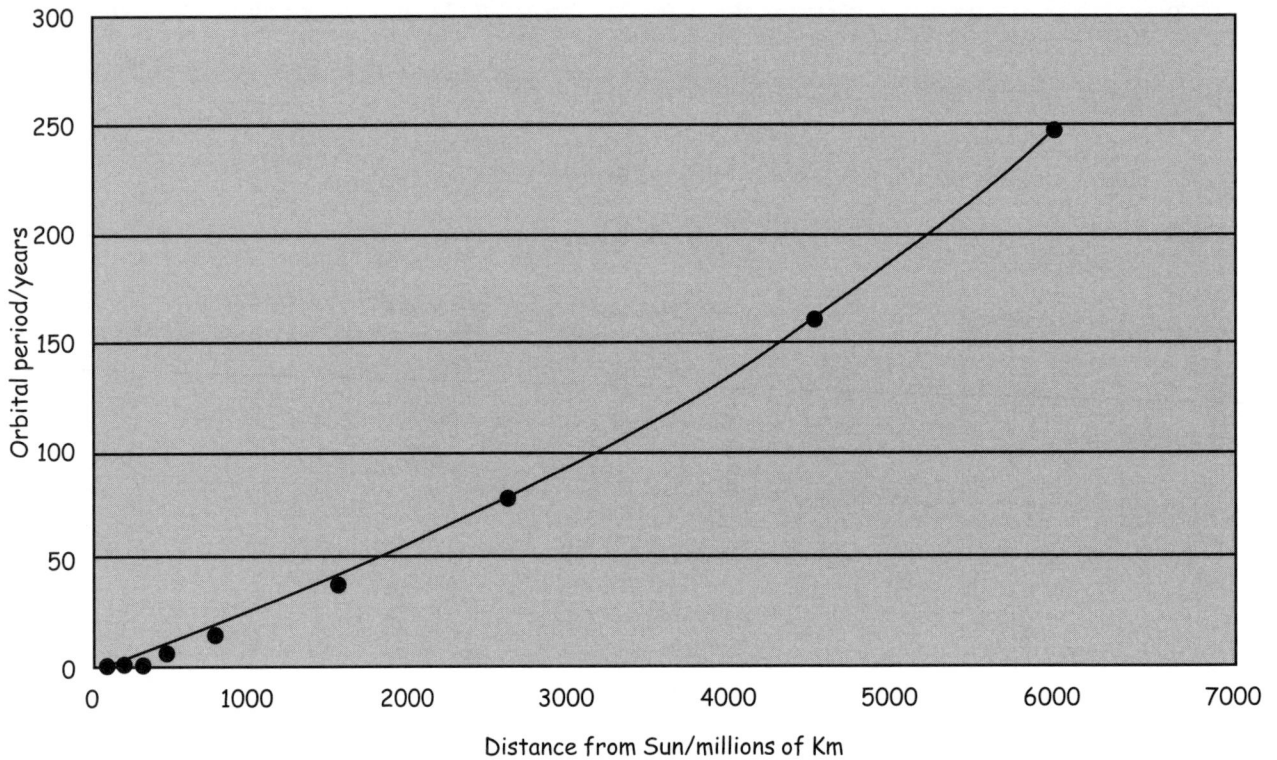

Planet	Distance from Sun millions of km	Orbital period (year length) years
Earth	149.6	1
Jupiter	778.3	11.9
Mars	227.9	1.88
Mercury	57.9	0.24
Neptune	4496.6	165
Pluto	5900	248
Saturn	1427	29.5
Uranus	2869.6	84
Venus	108.2	0.62

Data sheet 4

PUPIL SHEET

Comparison of number of moons with the planet's gravity force

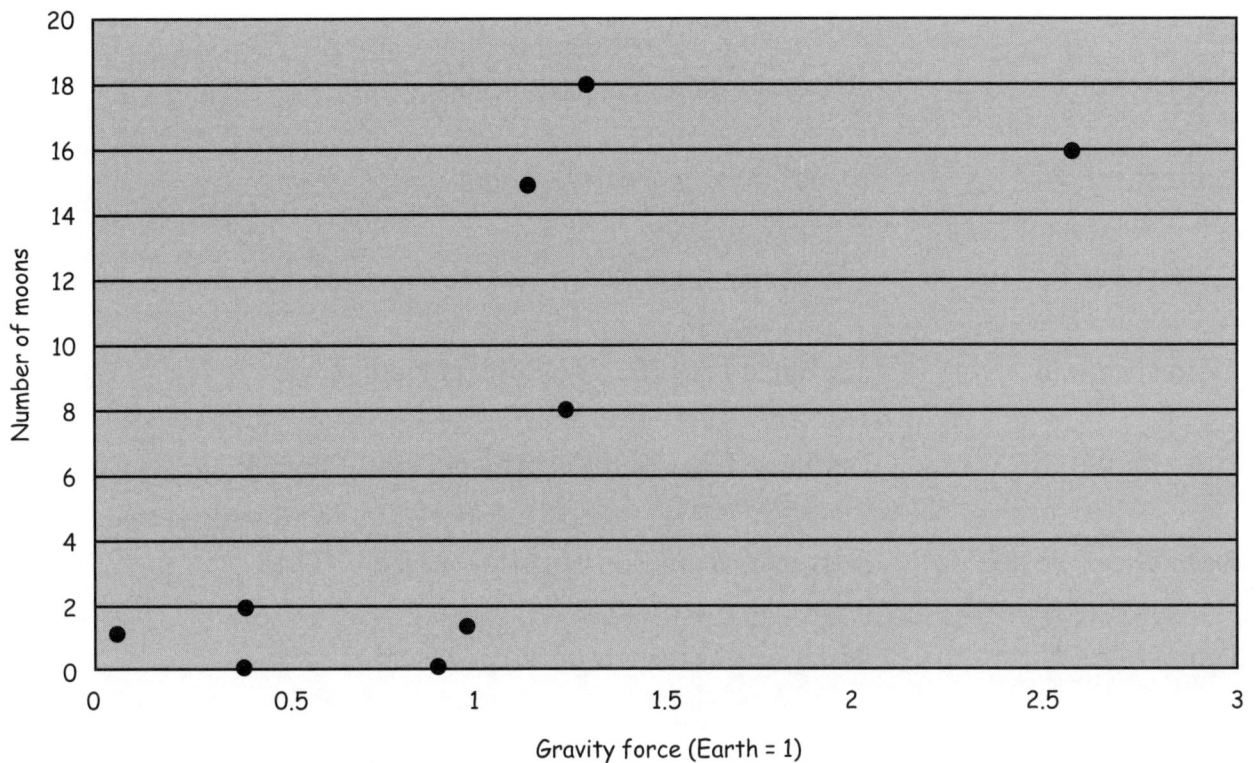

Planet	Gravity force, cf Earth	Number of moons
Earth	1	1
Jupiter	2.64	16
Mars	0.38	2
Mercury	0.38	0
Neptune	1.21	8
Pluto	0.06	1
Saturn	1.16	18
Uranus	1.11	15
Venus	0.9	0

Excel spreadsheets on the CDRom

Data sheet 1	Table 1: All data
Data sheet 1	Table 2: Planet type and atmosphere
Data sheet 2	Planet mass v gravity – Chart
Data sheet 2	Planet mass v gravity – Table
Data sheet 3a	Distance from Sun v orbital period – Chart A
Data sheet 3b	Distance from Sun v orbital period – Chart B
Data sheet 3a and 3b	Distance from Sun v orbital period – Table
Data sheet 4	Number of moons v gravity – Chart

Outline

Chromatography is an analytical tool which is widely used in industry. Pupils need to be able to link the simple practical work which they have done to the wider context and the wider evaluation processes which have to be undertaken. This exemplar attempts to do this while developing pupils' abilities to process and evaluate information. Pupils are required to interpret outputs from gas chromatograms to identify wrongdoers who have left behind forensic evidence at the scene. There are three scenarios or mysteries, which are similar, but vary in difficulty:

- **Mystery 1** looks at the analysis of oil from four garages to identify a burglar.
- **Mystery 2** looks at the analysis of four oils from different sources along with an analysis of reports of suspects' whereabouts to identify the wrongdoer.
- **Mystery 3** again looks at the analysis of oils. This time there is a wider range of samples and the possibility of experimental error has to be taken into account in working out possible suspects.

Pupils' prior knowledge and skills

Although chromatography is not in the Key Stage 2 Programme of Study, many pupils will have met the concept in primary school since it is a popular activity and is often addressed practically as the simple paper chromatography of ink. Before starting this exemplar, it would be useful if pupils had discussed paper chromatography and had carried out some further practical work in this connection – such as the analysis of red cabbage, beetroot or other leaf extracts. Gas liquid chromatography need not have been discussed prior to starting the exemplar as it will be dealt with in the introduction to the activities.

Links

QCA Scheme of Work	Thinking skills	Key scientific idea
Unit 7H Solutions Unit 8F Compounds and Mixtures	Information processing Evaluation	Particles

Lesson objectives

Thinking skills:
- sort and classify information
- consider what information needs to be evaluated to solve a problem
- evaluate information
- evaluate the degree of confidence that can be placed in the judgments made.

Science:
- recognise that experimental evidence can be used to evaluate scientific happenings in the past
- recognise that experimental evidence is limited by the accuracy of the instruments used, human error and the quality of the sample tested
- understand that the various uses of chromatography in its many forms include a diagnostic use in crime detection.

Context

This was carried out with Year 7 classes of differing abilities after work on paper chromatography which involved using discs of filter paper and felt tip pens. Pupils had also crushed up red cabbage and produced extract which they analysed by the same method. The work of Tswett in isolating the pigments in chlorophyll had been discussed and so the pupils knew of the use of chromatography in analysis. They had no knowledge of gas liquid chromatography (GLC) before they started this activity. The process was introduced as another type of chromatography used, as with the other forms, in analysis.

There is no need to go into the explanation of how GLC works. The exemplar concerns the use of the tool in diagnostic identification. Its use in quantitative investigation (area under the peaks/height of peaks) may be important in developing the science knowledge of some pupils, and indeed in developing further thinking skills in extension activities. It is not important, however, in the contexts which pupils will be using in this exemplar.

Not all groups did all three mysteries, which vary in difficulty. Where there was a mix of abilities in groups who did all three, some pupils found *Mystery 3*, for example, too hard and interest flagged. Interest had been quite high during the first two mysteries, so this may have been due, in part, to the length of the written introduction to *Mystery 3*. Here, a verbal introduction by the teacher to explain the scenario was found to help. Other pupils managed all three mysteries well and it was felt that they could have coped with, and enjoyed, even more difficult or ambiguous material that would have presented them with more cognitive conflict. There is no reason why you may not alter the materials to change the degree of difficulty presented to pupils. This will enhance both learning and thinking.

Mystery 2 needs pupils to take into account who should or could have had access to the various sites in conjunction with the chromatography evidence.

Mystery 3 highlights the problems caused by inaccurate tools and experimental errors. 0.5min inaccuracy in retention times leads to inconclusive deductions and prolongs the investigation.

Preparation

1 Decide which of the mysteries you will use. Normally, all the groups need to be set the same problem or series of problems and work their way through these. If not, then the plenary session can be difficult to organise. Because they have not experienced and discussed the same conflicts in the group work, pupils may not make the expected jumps in cognition. Not all mysteries need be attempted, but all in the same class should attempt the same number of mysteries.

2 Once you have decided which mysteries they will attempt, you should produce copies of the experimental results and the mysteries for each group of pupils.

Introduction

1 Most pupils are aware of the work of forensic scientists, (especially SOCO – scene of crime officers) through many television crime series like *Taggart, Morse, Dalziel and Pascoe* and *The Bill*. Introduce the exemplar by discussing the work of these TV officers. Ask pupils what they do and how they think that the officers arrive at their results.

2 It is important that pupils 'get in to' or try to be a 'fly on the wall' in each scenario by using their imagination. Once the task is known, it may be worth you trying to paint a picture of the scenario in words, especially in *Mystery 2*. You could produce a map on the board of the position of the various shops and the garage to make it more realistic.

3 Make sure that pupils are familiar with paper chromatography. They will be aware that this process can separate dye pigments into its separate components, depending on the dye and the solvent used. The activities work better if pupils know the basic principle of paper chromatography, ie that the distance moved by the dye depends on the resultant of the propelling forces (solubility) and the retarding or 'sticking' forces (the attraction of the paper will do – rather than trying to explain partition).

4 Follow this by introducing the process of gas/liquid chromatography. There is no need to go into the principles of gas liquid chromatography. The process can be explained as a direct comparison with paper chromatography: the flow of gas is the propelling force and the column 'filling' is responsible for the retarding forces. The material sample separated is not in this case dye, but can be mixtures of liquids like oil or other chemicals. The detection can be explained like a paper chromatogram that has been left in the liquid too long and all the dye has moved to the edge of the paper, arriving at different times due to the amount of 'drag'. When it eventually arrives at the end of the column, although it can't be seen, it can be detected in some way. As the graph paper moves through the detector at a regular rate, the different materials cause the pen to rise and fall as they are detected and so the paper shows a series of peaks as the different materials come out of the end

GLC can be introduced to pupils as a fully automated type of chromatography which is used widely in industry, such as in the identification of the percentage of alcohol in the blood in drink driving cases.

of the column. Different mixtures of chemicals give a different series of peaks.

5 Give the pupils a sample quantity/time output graph (page 118). Ensure that pupils can interpret the tables of results, linking them to what the output graph would have looked like. Alternatively, you may draw the output graph for each mystery, if you feel that this is necessary. This can be given to pupils as a handout instead of the tables. With one class where this was done, it was felt that the more visual evidence (graphs) helped the pupils.

6 The time units (mins x10) were chosen to minimise problems arising from decimal fractions of a minute. Pupils need to be able to understand the relevance of the time units. Explain this to pupils, or, alternatively, takethem as 'time units'.

7 Finally, you should go over the mystery as outlined on the pupil worksheet, to be sure that pupils understand clearly the nature of the mystery, what they are expected to do and what answers they are expected to bring to the plenary discussion.

8 Once the task is fully understood divide pupils into groups of three or four to carry out their investigations and evaluate the evidence.

(T) To sort and classify information.

(T) To consider what information needs to be evaluated to solve a problem.

(T) To evaluate information, leading to metacognition.

(T) To evaluate the degree of confidence that can be placed in the judgements made.

Group work

Groups should consider and discuss all the evidence available, including the non-forensic evidence in *Mystery 2*. In *Mystery 3* they need to take account of possible experimental error. Pupils should come to a conclusion in their groups, consider how confident they are of their conclusion, and bring the results of their deliberations to the plenary session. While they are working, carry out class scans to identify issues and the order in which you will take group contributions in the plenary. Making notes may help.

Plenary

Lead a whole class discussion of the group decisions and their reasoning. While you are doing class scans, select which groups will illustrate the issues they are raising, and work out the order in which you will ask the groups to report back. The most popular choices need to be identified and their reasons understood. Suspects should not be identified without a reason! Discuss different choices of suspect, along with the incriminating evidence, and the level of confidence the pupils have about that selection. The whole class should then arrive at a consensus as to which suspect has perpetrated the crime! Possible issues that may arise in discussion are outlined on the *Possible Outcomes* teacher sheet.

Follow-up

More difficult mysteries and scenarios can be designed, but the three problems in themselves represent a progression in difficulty.

Thinking Skills Through Science

Possible outcomes

TEACHER SHEET

MYSTERY 1

D – also at garage 1

A – also at garage 1

B

MYSTERY 2

June was arrested!

Jim had been in the bakery, garage, bicycle shop - all legitimate and checked.

Fred had been in the garage and the bakery - both legitimate and checked.

Gemma had been in the bicycle shop, garage and builders' merchant - all checked.

June had been in the builders' merchant and garage (checked). But also in the bakery. But according to the evidence, she should not have been there!

MYSTERY 3

(1)

Most popular G, second most popular J.

Least popular A, H, I.

Least sure about C – only one peak to compare with.

(2)

Yes.

Not alone (no peak at around 10).

E is identified from both samples, as is C. But because of there only being one peak by which to identify it, and because one of the other oils contains a peak at 80, this is much less certain. Note that sample 1 identifies oil D, but sample 2 does not, so it is eliminated. Sample 2 identifies A but sample 1 does not. Sample 2 does not identify J because J has two peaks (identifying two compounds) at 25 and 35.

Mystery 1

Typical sample of a gas liquid chromatograph

Peaks shown at approximately 25, 30, 40, 45 and 55 (mins x 10)

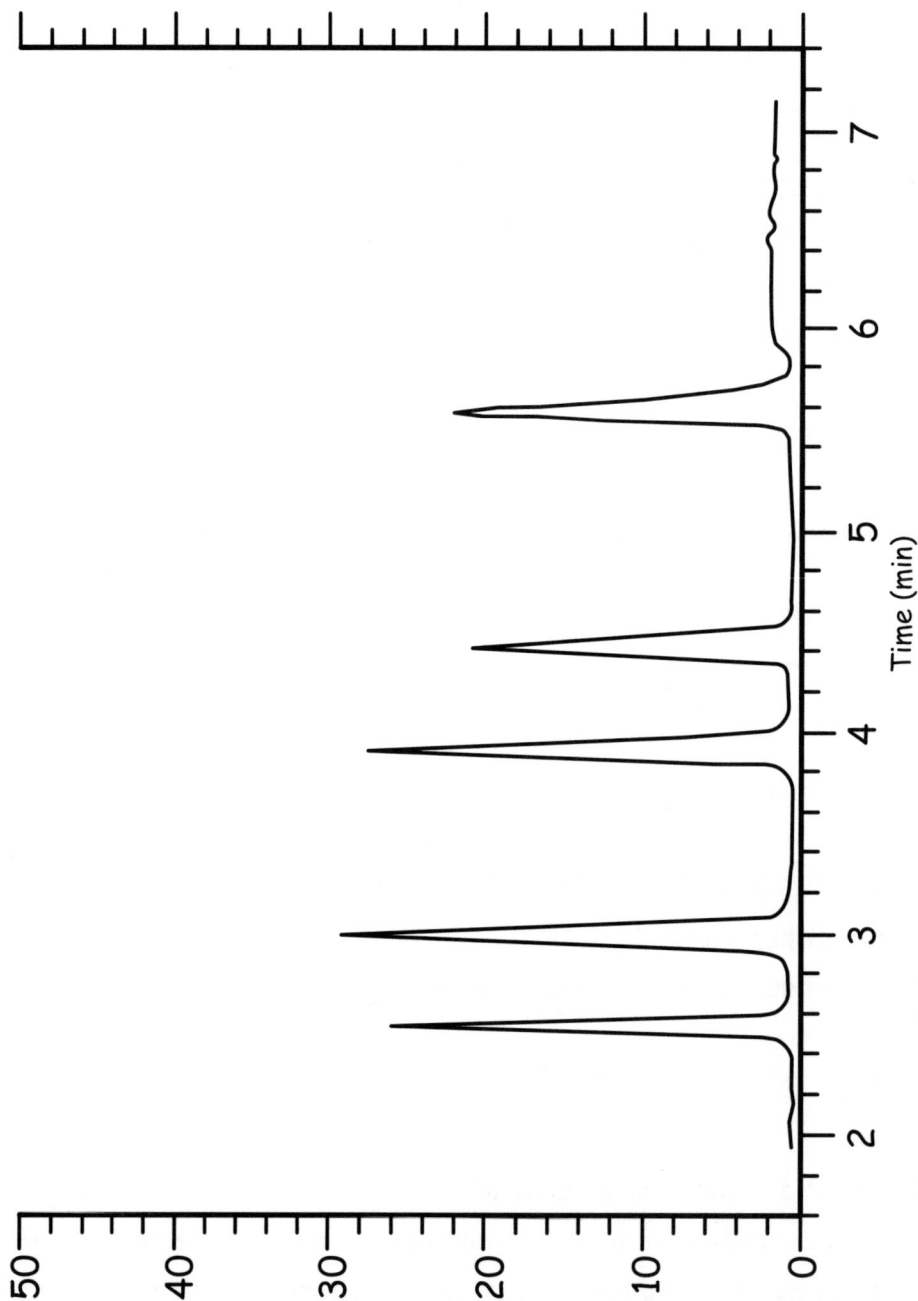

Thinking Skills Through Science

Mystery 1   PUPIL SHEET 2

Four garages fix peoples' cars and service them. They all use different makes of oil, which they put into cars when they service them.

Garage 1 has oil which gives chromatogram peaks at 2 and 7 minutes.

Garage 2 has oil which gives chromatogram peaks at 2, 3 and 6 minutes.

Garage 3 has oil which gives chromatogram peaks at 1 and 4 minutes.

Garage 4 has oil which gives chromatogram peaks at 3, 4 and 7 minutes.

One day there is a series of burglaries from the garages and money is stolen from the owners. The burglars walk over the garage floors in every case.

Police arrest four suspects. The oil on their shoes is tested.

The oil from suspect A gives peaks at 1, 2, 4 and 7 minutes.

The oil from suspect B gives peaks at 2, 3, 4 and 7 minutes.

The oil from suspect C gives peaks at 1, 3 and 7 minutes.

The oil from suspect D gives peaks at 2, 3, 6 and 7 minutes.

Q1. Which suspect could have stolen from garage 2?

Q2. Where else could this suspect have been?

Q3. Which suspect could have stolen from garage 3?

Q4. Where else has this suspect been?

Q5. Who could have stolen from both garage 1 and garage 4?

Mystery 2   PUPIL SHEET

Four shops sell different kinds of oil. The garage sells oil for cars. The bicycle shop sells lubricating oil for bikes. The baker's shop sells cooking oil and the builders' merchant sells creosote oil for protecting wooden fences. Traces of these oils are to be found on the shop floor in each case.

Analysis of the four types of oil gives the following results:

Oil	Peaks at the following times (minsx10)
Car oil	10, 40
Lubricating oil	20, 60
Cooking oil	50
Creosote	30, 40

Jim, the baker's boy delivers bread in the street on his bike.

Fred, the garage mechanic works 9-5 and always stops fixing cars between 12 and 1 so that he can eat his sandwich, which he buys from the baker's shop every day.

Gemma, who works in the bicycle shop, has a little car which she parks in the garage, off the road, every day (she is a friend of the garage owner, who lets her do this free).

June works at the builders' merchant and she goes out with Fred at the garage (they eat lunch together at the garage – Fred always goes and buys her a sandwich along with his own).

One day, the baker's shop is broken into and a sum of money is stolen. Police are called and they ask Jim, Fred, Gemma and June some questions.

It turns out that Gemma says that during the previous day, she parked her car at the garage as usual and saw very few customers all day. The only local one she remembers was Jim who came in for some oil for his bike. Fred and June had been at work all day and each said that they had eaten lunch together at the garage (their usual sandwiches from the baker's). Jim had seen them when he came in on his bike for a packet of crisps, which Fred had sold him. June said that Gemma had come in just before lunchtime and bought some creosote for her fence at home. Fred confirmed that she had taken the container to her car after lunch, before going back to work.

Police took samples from all of their shoes and carried out a chromatographic analysis of them using gas liquid chromatography. The results are shown below:

Suspect	Peaks at the following times (minsx10)
Jim	10, 20, 40, 50, 60
Fred	10, 40, 50
Gemma	10, 20, 30, 40, 60
June	10, 30, 40, 50

Q1. Who did the police arrest, and why?

Mystery 3 PUPIL SHEET

Some garages only sell their own make of oil. Others can keep whichever oils they want to sell. In Anytown, overall, ten motorcar oils are available for garages to sell to their customers.

A survey of oils is carried out by Anytown High School who have been given an old gas liquid chromatogram by a local firm, who have bought a new up to date one for themselves. Although old, the GLC works well. However, the packing in the column is not perfect and the school finds it difficult to keep the gas pressure constant. This, together with the fact that the pupils are not expert at carrying out the testing, means that the results are not as accurate as perhaps they could be. An error of about plus or minus half a minute (5 time units = 5minsx10) needs to be taken into account when comparing results. So a sample that should give a peak at 50 could give a peak anywhere between 45 and 55.

The oils, when tested, give GLC peaks at the following times from injection:

Oil	Peaks at the following times (minsx10)
A	25, 60
B	10, 20, 30
C	80
D	70, 90
E	10, 30, 50
F	45, 65
G	30, 80
H	55, 95
I	20, 40, 60
J	25, 35, 85

These oils A to J were tested three times and are the correct standard peak values for each of the oils against which the field samples are checked. You can thus assume that there are no reading errors in these standard values, although there may be errors in the field sample readings.

Mystery 3 continued   PUPIL SHEET

Pupils from the school split into four groups and each collects a sample of oil from an area in the town. On return to school, they test the samples, which give the following results:

Oil from site	Peaks at the following times (minsx10)
1	10, 20, 30, 45, 70, 85
2	30, 40, 70, 80
3	10, 30, 45, 80
4	10, 20, 35, 75, 90

Q1. Which oils are most and second most popular?

Q2. Which oils appear never to have been used at any site?

Q3. Which oil are you least sure about? Why?

Two diamond robberies were carried out in Anytown. After investigation, the police came up with two suspects. Two samples of oil were picked up from the road at the site of the robberies. The oil from the suspects' cars was also tested (the cars were old and oil was leaking from them). Pupils from the school tested the oil samples.

Oil from site	Peaks at the following times (minsx10)
1	15, 35, 50, 75, 90
2	10, 30, 55, 80, 95
Oil from car of suspect	Peaks at the following times (minsx10)
a	35, 80
b	50, 95

Q4. Could these suspects have been involved in the robbery?

Q5. Could they have done it themselves?

Q6. What oil or oils could you tell the police to be on the look out for in the car of anyone else involved?

Q7. How sure could you be about this information?

Variation in Humans

T Some pupils will understand relationships primarily through a visual representation.

Outline

In this exemplar pupils use measurements of a range of different characteristics of human beings to identify possible relationships between them. The relationships are most accessible through the visual representation in a scattergram. Many pupils do not see the relationships in graphs that teachers might assume, so this activity addresses this by providing both tables and scattergrams (with and without trend lines). There are associated Excel files on the CDRom if that is easier to use.

Links with numeracy across the curriculum.

Pupils' prior knowledge and skills

Pupils do not learn about variation in Key Stage 2 although primary schools often use measurements of parts of the body as a context for developing measuring and recording skills.

Pupils will need to be familiar with interpreting graphs to identify relationships. They will also find it helpful to be able to identify an anomalous result on a graph.

Links

QCA Scheme of Work	Thinking skills	Key scientific idea
Unit 7D Variation and Classification	Information processing Evaluation	Interdependence

Lesson objectives

Thinking skills:
- collect, sort and analyse data to identify relationships (information processing)
- decide on relevant and irrelevant data when looking at trends.

Science:
- describe some ways individual human beings vary from each other.

Context

T It is important not to let the mathematics get in the way of the science or thinking.

The exemplar was carried out with middle-ability Year 7 classes and also as an introduction to Unit 9A Inheritance and Selection with Year 9 middle-ability classes. Pupils measured their height, hand span, arm span, shoe size and the circumference of their heads and recorded them in a chart. They then graphed them before analysing the data. Other groups used the tables and graphs provided. Some pupils used the Excel scattergrams directly, having access to ICT resources.

Although they found it an enjoyable activity, those who used their own results found graphing the results difficult and time consuming and the whole activity took too long. By the time they had got to the whole point of the lesson – analysing the data – their motivation had decreased somewhat. When pupils were presented with graphed data which had previously been collected and collated and asked to identify relationships from it, they spent much more time analysing the data and developed both thinking skills and science understanding at a much greater pace. The analysis was more successful with Year 9 pupils than it had been with Year 7.

Preparation

If suitable ICT facilities are available pupils can print out their own graphs, or work with the graphs on the computer. This also gives opportunities to change the scales of the graphs to help to search out relationships.

1 Divide pupils into groups. Working in this way aids speculation and discussion of possible relationships. Decide whether to group according to ability or otherwise.
2 The data is stored on the associated Excel spreadsheet and tables and scattergrams of different pairs of measurements are available. Some graphs have trend lines drawn on, some do not. You should decide whether to present these as hard copy or allow pupils to access them on computers themselves. Giving pupils the chance to collect, present and graph their own results is not recommended, as it detracts from the main objectives of the activity. Only if you feel that they need practice should you do this – but probably not in the same lesson.

3 Pupils need to be able to identify when there is a correlation between the two quantities shown in the graph: they will recognise a regular pattern. You may wish to practice this skill as described in the following *Introduction*.

Introduction

1 Use a starter activity to tune pupils in to interpreting graphs and identifying those that show a correlation. Use an OHT showing different examples of graphs – some that do show a relationship and some that don't. Everyday examples work well. Include those that pupils can identify with, such as the amount of pocket money against age, the number of fast food outlets in a town compared with the number of cinemas, the number of TVs and the number of children in a home. If there is a relationship, pupils give a 'thumbs up' sign; if not 'thumbs down'. Pupils should then explain what the relationship is.

2 Give each group a set of graphs and a series of questions to answer, eg what happens to finger length/arm span/shoe size/head circumference as the height increases?

3 Remind pupils about the rules of group work, especially the requirement to have an agreed group answer to the question, so that it can be discussed at the plenary.

> (T) The starter activity enables the teacher to get a quick picture of those pupils who grasp the concept quickly and those that do not.

> (T) Many pupils were reluctant to say when there was no obvious relationship.

Group work

Pupils worked in small groups of two to four. Assigning different sets of data for investigation to different groups speeded up the analysis and allowed some differentiation. At least two groups were given the same data to analyse but most groups had no more than two sets. This enabled discussion to take place between the groups with the same data and allowed other groups to question them during feedback. However, depending on the ability of the groups, you may wish to give all groups the same questions to analyse, in order that all pupils have had the same experience in the group work.

If it was clear that a group of pupils could not make progress because they could not identify whether there was a correlation or not, the graph with a trend line was given as supplementary information.

Use the information from class scans to stage-manage the plenary session.

Plenary

During the class scans you will probably find that different groups of pupils have different opinions regarding the correlation of the sets of data. During the plenary, ask groups which hold different views to justify their decisions. Then ask the class to agree whether there is a definite correlation or not.

> (T) Thinking skills – pupils need to sort through the data to identify trends.

Discussion of the overall outcomes will be more focused if you produce a summary on the board of the pairs of data and the decisions reached by the groups. As a part of the plenary this will help to review the lesson objectives. Asking pupils to collaboratively agree a single statement about variation in human beings will provide a useful summary of pupils' understanding and encourage them to review their learning.

The plenary discussion and the production of the single statement are likely to be the points at which there is most cognitive challenge. You need to fuel the discussion as far as possible. Understanding the potential relationships between variables is a foundation of good science.

Resources

The following charts are available as photocopiable masters, or on the CDRom as Excel spreadsheets for you to download and print off or use directly on computers.

Charts
1   Shoe size compared with hand span
2   Hand span compared with height
3   Arm span compared with hand span
4   Shoe size compared with arm span
5   Circumference of head compared with shoe size
6   Circumference of head compared with height
7   Arm span compared with height
8   Shoe size compared with height
9   Circumference of head compared with hand span
10   Circumference of head compared with arm span

Charts with trend line
1   Shoe size compared with hand span
2   Hand span compared with height
3   Arm span compared with hand span
4   Shoe size compared with arm span
5   Circumference of head compared with shoe size
6   Circumference of head compared with height
7   Arm span compared with height
8   Shoe size compared with height
9   Circumference of head compared with hand span
10   Circumference of head compared with arm span

Table 1: Data tables of variations

PUPIL SHEET

Variations

Shoe size compared with hand span

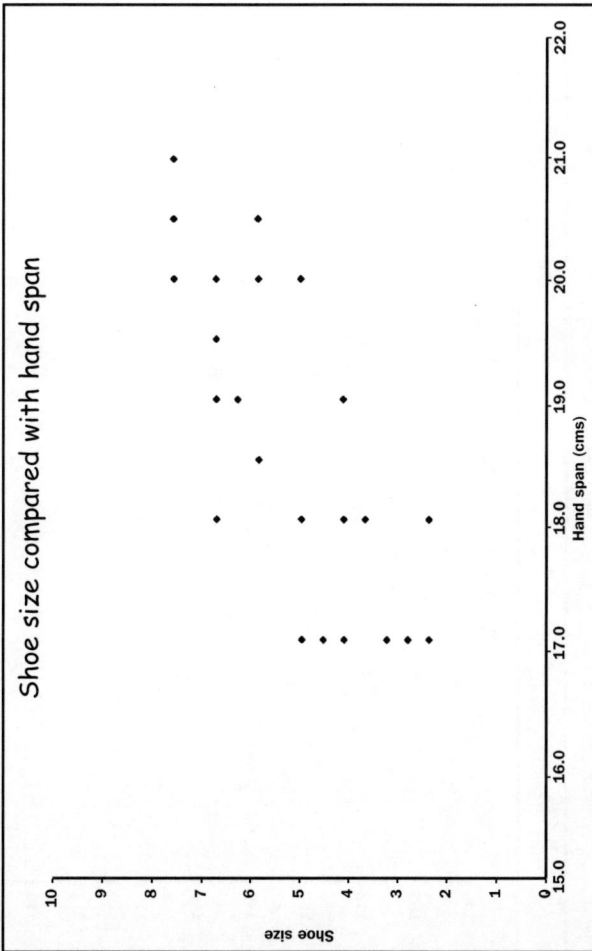

Arm span compared with hand span

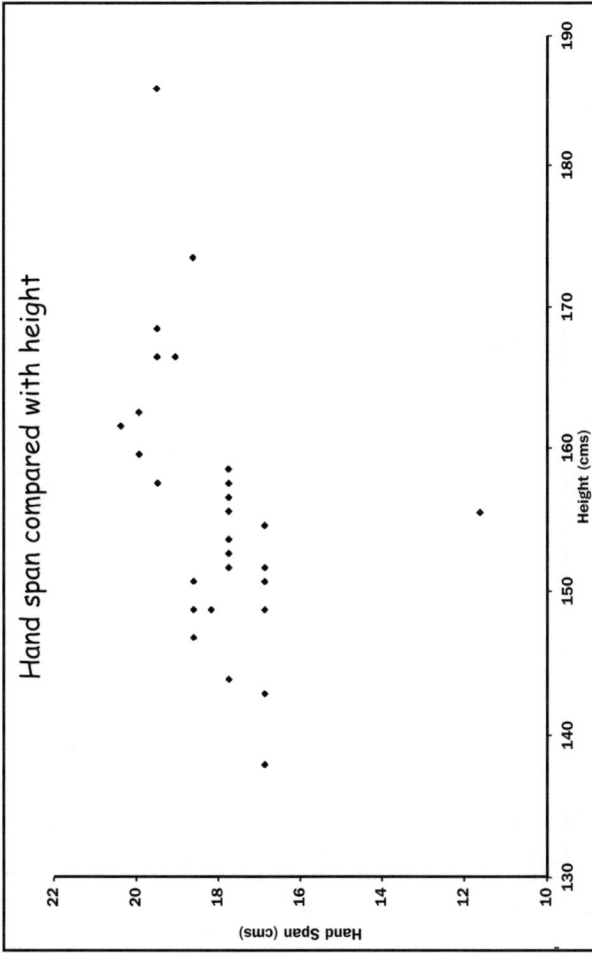

Hand span compared with height

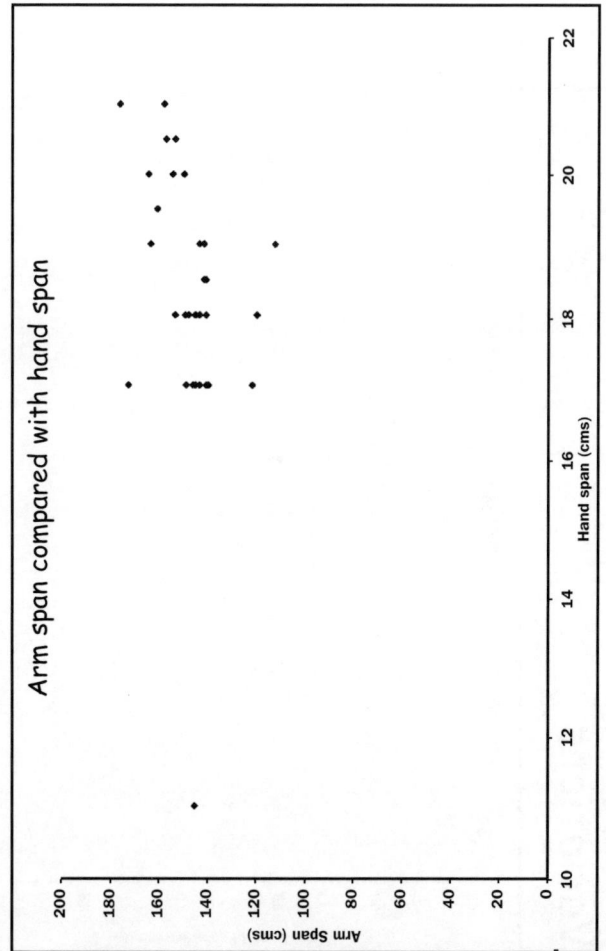

Shoe size compared with arm span

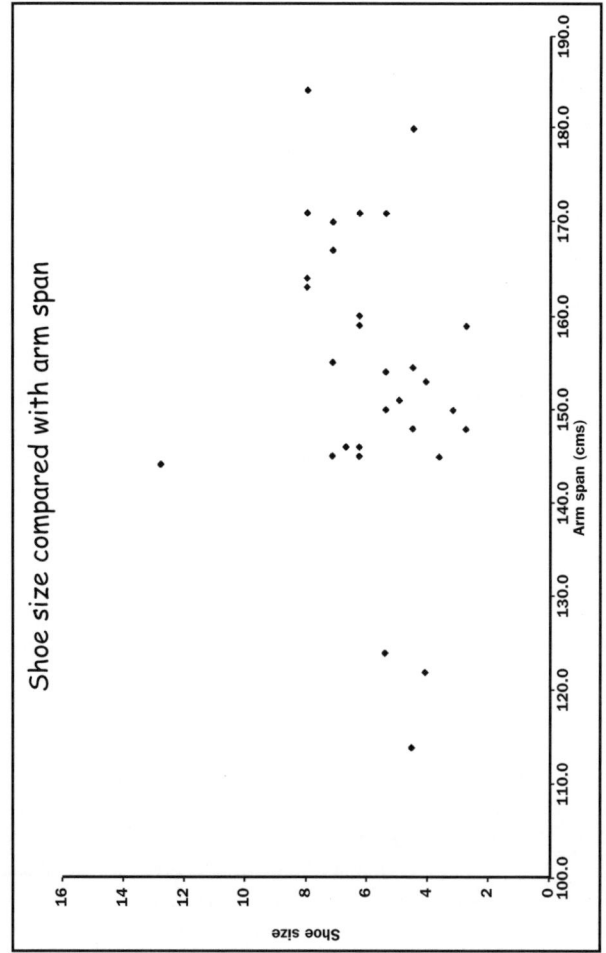

PUPIL SHEET

Variations

Circumference of head compared with shoe size

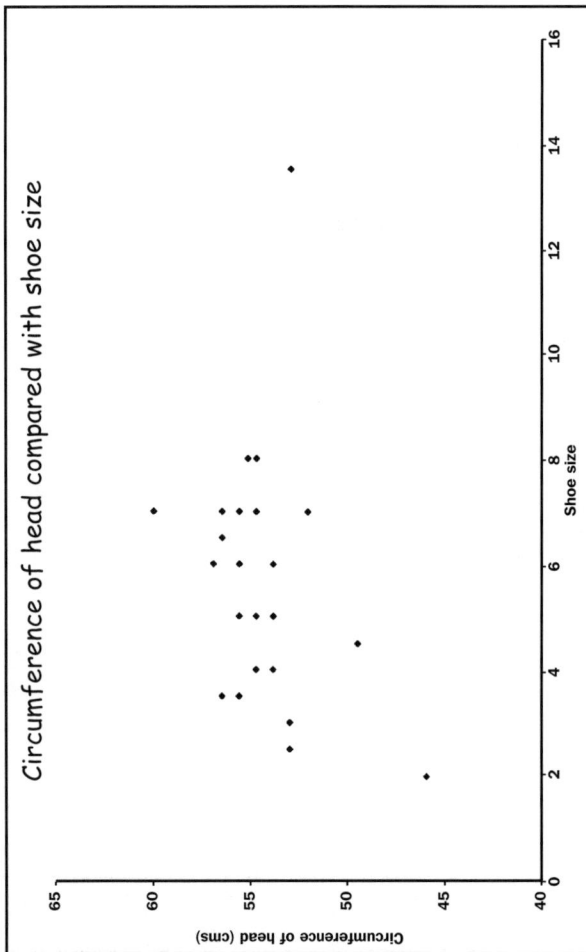

Circumference of head compared with height

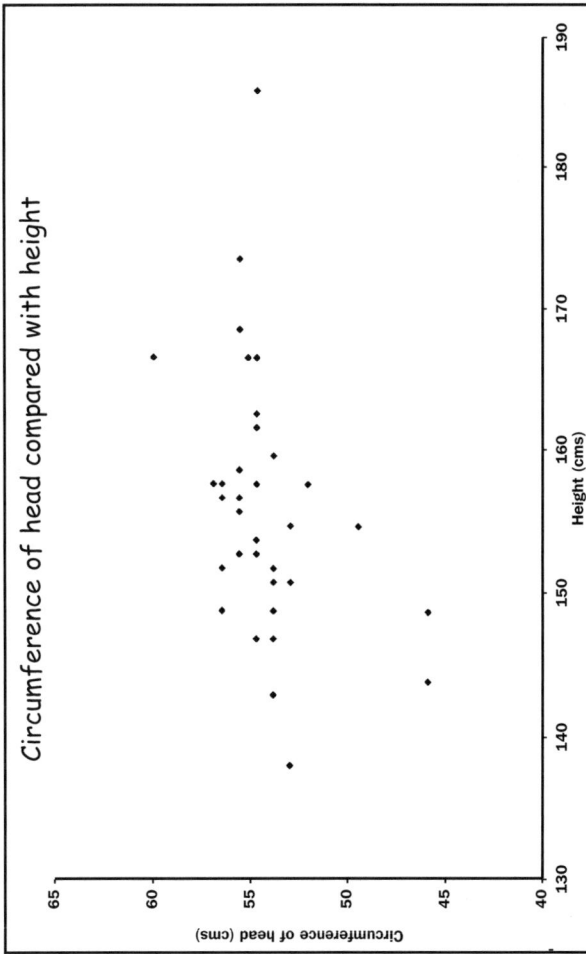

Arm span compared with height

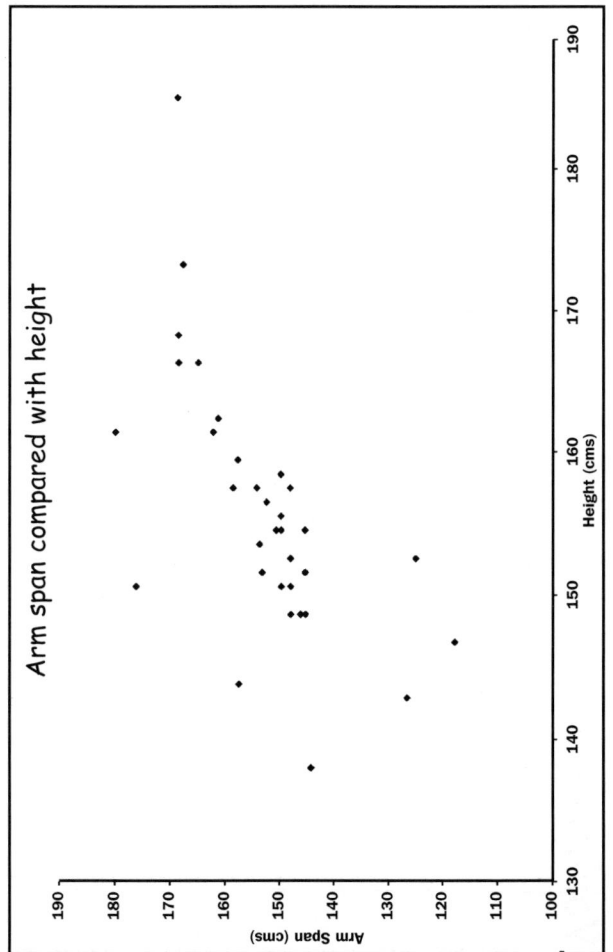

Shoe size compared with height

Variations

PUPIL SHEET

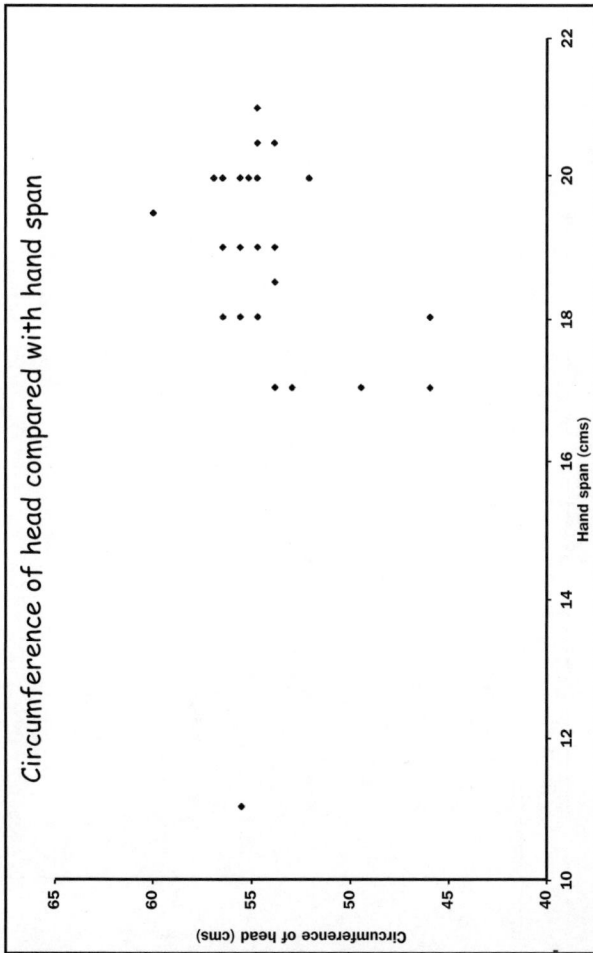

Circumference of head compared with hand span

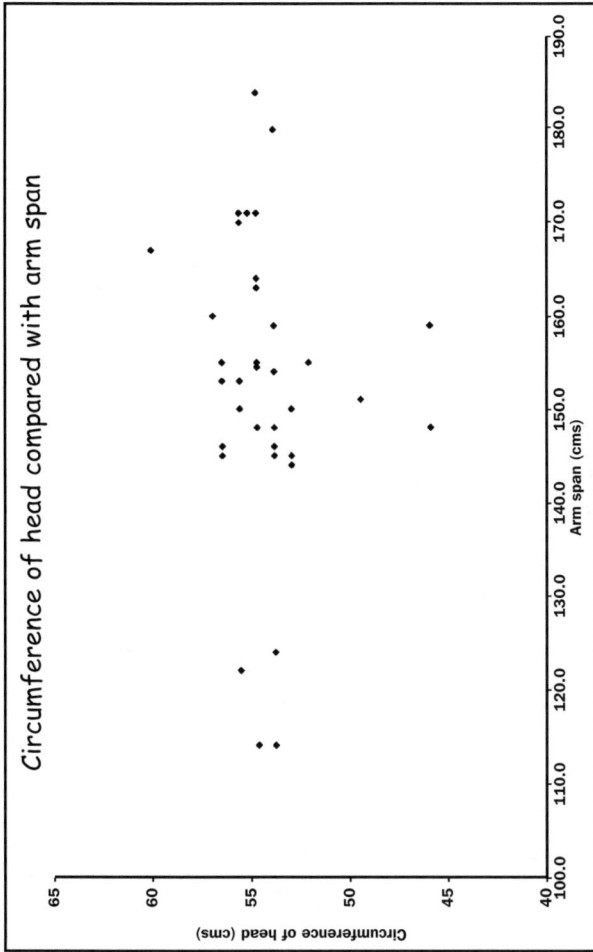

Circumference of head compared with arm span

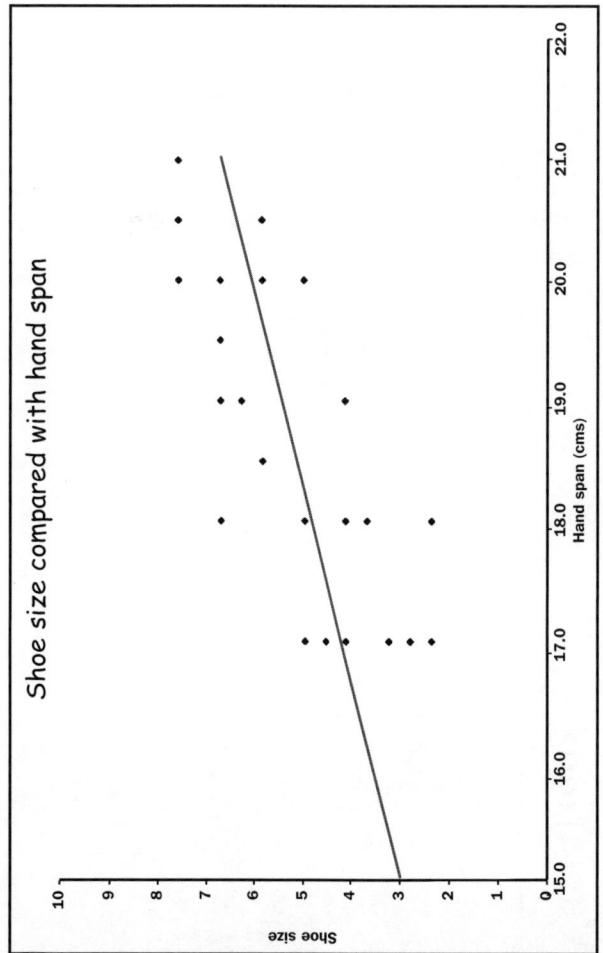

Shoe size compared with hand span

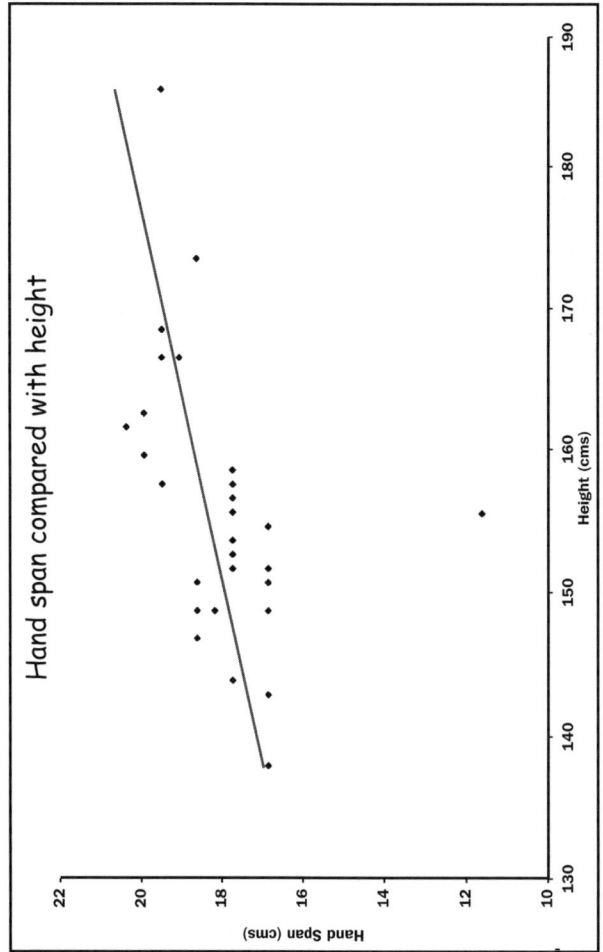

Hand span compared with height

Variations

Arm span compared with hand span

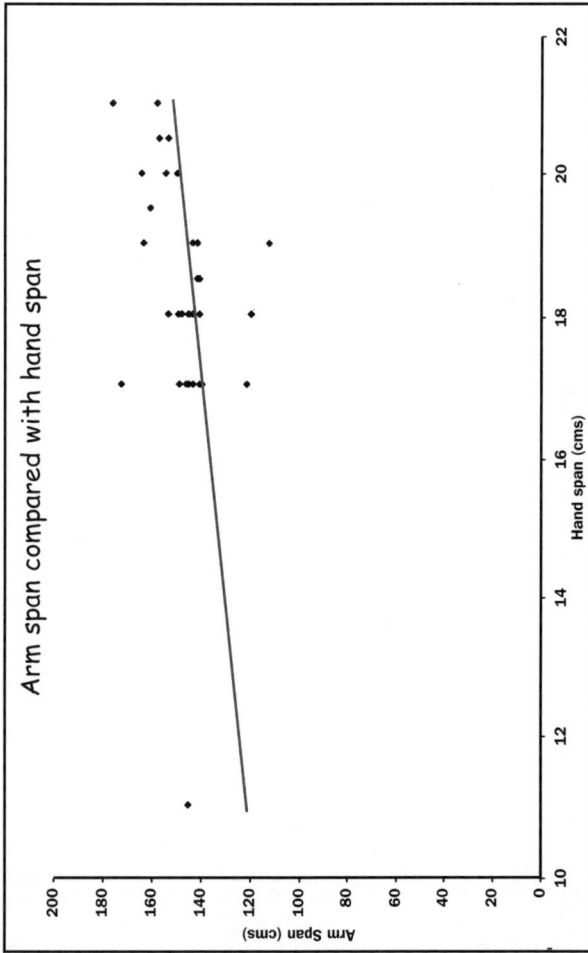

Shoe size compared with arm span

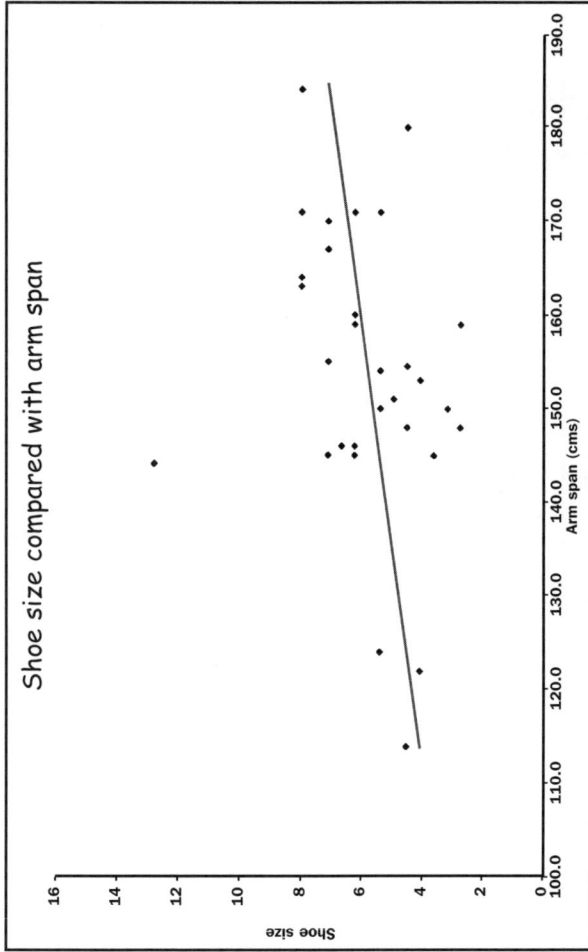

Circumference of head compared with shoe size

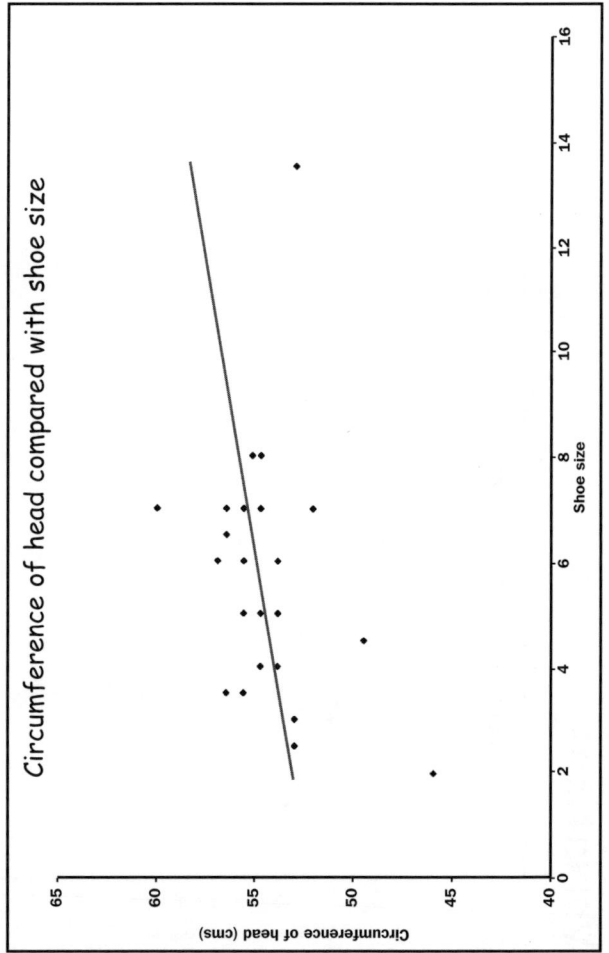

Circumference of head compared with height

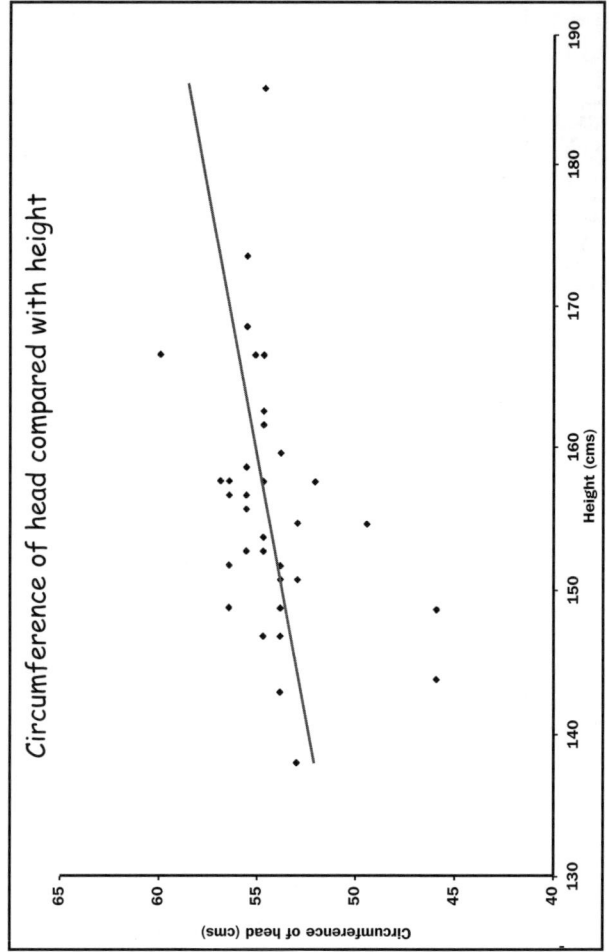

Variations

PUPIL SHEET

Arm span compared with height

Shoe size compared with height

Circumference of head compared with hand span

Circumference of head compared with arm span

PUPIL SHEET

Variations

Height (cms)	Hand Span (cms)	Arm span (cms)	Shoe size	Circumference of head (cms)	Hair colour	Eye colour	Tongue roller
149	19.0	146.0	6.5	57.0	brown	green	Yes
174	19.0	170.0	7	56.0	brown	blue	Yes
152	17.0	154.0	5	54.0	blonde	blue	Yes
152	18.0	145.0	7	57.0	blonde	blue	Yes
163	20.5	163.0	8	55.0	brown	blue	Yes
158	20.0	155.0	7	57.0	brown	brown	Yes
162	21.0	164.0	8	55.0	brown	brown	Yes
149	18.5	146.0	6	54.0	brown	brown	Yes
158	20.0	160.0	6	57.5	brown	brown	no
153	18.0	148.0	4	55.0	blonde	blue	Yes
147	19.0	114.0	4	55.0	brown	blue	Yes
186	20.0	171.0	8	55.0	brown	green	Yes
156	11.0	150.0	5	56.0	brown	blue	no
158	20.0	155.0	7	52.0	brown	blue	Yes
167	19.5	167.0	7	61.0	brown	green	Yes
155	17.0	145.0	3	53.0	brown	brown	Yes
155	17.0	150.0	2.5	53.0	blonde	blue	Yes
149	17.0	148.0	2	45.0	blonde	blue	Yes
160	20.5	159.0	6	54.0	brown	blue	Yes
157	18.0	153.0	3.5	56.0	brown	brown	Yes
155	17.0	151.0	4.5	49.0	brown	green	Yes
138	17.0	144.0	13.5	53.0	brown	green	Yes
149	18.5	145.0	6	54.0	blonde	green	no
169	20.0	171.0	6	56.0	brown	brown	Yes
153	18.0	122.0	3.5	56.0	brown	blue	Yes
153	18.0	122.0	3.5	56.0	brown	blue	Yes
143	17.0	124.0	5	54.0	brown	blue	no
151	17.0	180.0	4	54.0	blonde	blue	Yes
154	18.0	154.5	4	55.0	blonde	green	Yes
153	18.0	122.0	3.5	56.0	blonde	blue	Yes
144	18.0	159.0	2	45.0	blonde	blue	Yes
167	19.5	167.0	7	61.0	brown	blue	no
158	20.0	160.0	6	57.5	brown	brown	Yes
147	19.0	114.0	4	54.0	black	green	Yes
159	18.0	150.0	5	56.0	brown	blue	Yes
167	19.5	167.0	7	61.0	black	blue	no
158	20.0	160.0	6	57.5	blonde	blue	Yes
153	18.0	148.0	4	55.0	blonde	blue	Yes
147	19.0	114.0	4	55.0	red	green	Yes

PUPIL SHEET

Variations

Height (cms)	Hand Span (cms)	Arm span (cms)	Shoe size	Circumference of head (cms)	Hair colour	Eye colour	Tongue roller
151	19.0	148.0	4	54.0	blonde	blue	Yes
158	20.0	155.0	7	55.0	red	green	Yes
156	18.0	150.0	5	56.0	blonde	green	no
156	18.0	150.0	5	56.0	brown	blue	Yes
151	19.0	148.0	4	54.0	brown	brown	Yes
163	20.5	163.0	8	55.0	black	blue	no
158	20.0	155.0	7	57.0	brown	blue	no
162	21.0	184.0	8	55.0	blonde	blue	Yes
153	18.0	148.0	4	55.0	brown	brown	Yes
147	19.0	114.0	4	54.0	blonde	blue	no
151	17.0	150.0	2.5	53.0	brown	brown	Yes
155	17.0	151.0	4.5	49.0	brown	brown	no
155	17.0	145.0	3	53.0	brown	green	Yes
149	17.0	148.0	2	45.0	brown	blue	Yes
158	20.0	160.0	6	57.5	black	green	Yes
147	19.0	114.0	4	55.0	brown	green	no
149	19.0	146.0	6.5	57.0	brown	green	no
153	18.0	148.0	4	55.0	brown	brown	Yes
147	19.0	114.0	4	55.0	brown	blue	Yes
156	18.0	150.0	5	56.0	brown	blue	Yes
158	20.0	155.0	7	57.0	blonde	blue	Yes
167	20.0	171.0	5	55.0	blonde	green	Yes
158	18.0	148.0	4	55.0	brown	green	Yes
167	20.0	171.0	8	55.5	brown	blue	Yes
156	18.0	150.0	5	56.0	blonde	blue	Yes
149	18.5	145.0	6	54.0			
160	20.5	159.0	6	54.0			
153	18.0	122.0	3.5	56.0			
151	17.0	150.0	2.5	53.0			
157	18.0	153.0	3.5	57.0			
169	20.0	171.0	6	56.0			
153	18.0	148.0	4	55.0			
147	19.0	114.0	4	55.0			
163	20.5	163.0	8	55.0			
158	20.0	155.0	7	57.0			
162	21.0	164.0	8	55.0			

(T) This is another activity which forces hard thinking and provides a link between science and philosophy through argument.

Outline

Conversations with pupils and indeed with many adults reveal an almost bewildering array of what they believe constitutes 'science'. For example, many people think that astrology is a science and even surveys of postgraduate science students have shown that many believe you can prove an hypothesis! In this exemplar pupils are asked to evaluate statements about what science is. There are three possible activities:

1. Questionnaire *Is this a science?*
2. Card sort activity *Views about science*
3. *Controversial statements about science.*

You should choose the one most appropriate for your pupils. The intended outcome is that pupils have a greater understanding of what science is about, and how scientific study is carried out. The exemplar could be used in conjunction with other exemplars such as *Alternative Science Theories* (page 26) or *Climate Change* (page 44).

Pupils' prior knowledge and skills

During Key Stage 2 pupils learn about a wide range of phenomena. They begin to make links between ideas and to explain things using simple models and theories. During Key Stage 3 pupils build on these ideas and get a better idea of how science works. The choice of activity will be influenced by your pupils' experience of ideas and evidence in science.

Links

QCA Scheme of Work	Thinking skills	Key scientific ideas
There is no one particular unit to which this is linked, though a number of units in Years 7, 8 and 9 are relevant.	Reasoning Evaluation	All key ideas

Lesson objectives

Thinking skills:
- make judgements and decisions informed by evidence
- make deductions
- evaluate information
- develop criteria for judging the value of information.

Science:
- know about the nature of scientific knowledge and scientific activity
- reflect on how theories are generated
- consider the relationships between observations and theory.

Context

The nature of science and the development of scientific theories have not always received the explicit attention they deserve in Key Stage 3. Perhaps for this reason, some classes in Years 7, 8 and 9 struggled to find a clear purpose to these activities. It may be useful therefore to use one or two examples of the questions or statements provided in this exemplar to provide pupils with some guidance from the start as to how the discussion might proceed. Do this before you begin any work in groups.

The activities were most successful with higher-attaining groups who were used to thinking at a high level.

Biased views in any field are sometimes caused by exposure to one side of an argument only. These activities seek to get pupils to consider 'both sides of the penny' – the 'pros' and the 'cons'. There are some interesting issues that can crop up during the activities. For example:

- Does science tell us the truth?

- How do we tell the difference between science and non-science?
- If one group of scientists says that genetically modified foods are harmless and another says they are dangerous, whom should we believe?

The great value of science is that:

- scientific theories go far beyond the observable effects and speak about particles too small to see, or huge movements too slow to feel
- they (theories) suggest a mechanism for the effect, ie how it happens
- they stimulate new experiments by making predictions about them
- they can change.

(T) These may be some of the points that you would want to bring out of discussion at the end of the plenary.

Thus in 1981 in Arkansas where Creationists were arguing for equal time for 'creation-science' with Darwin's *Theory of Evolution*, their opponents quoted from the Creationists' most popular book:

However, this issue has re-surfaced recently with press reports of creationist teaching in some schools.

'We do not know how God created, what processes He used, for God used processes which are not now operating anywhere in the natural universe. This is why we refer to divine creation as special creation. We cannot discover by scientific investigation anything about creative processes…'

Q.E.D. Solomon (1983)

Preparation

1 Organise pupils into groups of between three and six. It is probably best to ensure an even mix of attainment within each group.
2 If a class has not taken part in this sort of activity before, you may need to consider whether to start with a general discussion about what pupils think science is, or what activities they might class as science. This will provide working background knowledge for them to use in making decisions about the statements or questions.
3 Decide which of the three possible activities you are going to use.
4 Photocopy sufficient copies of the questionnaire for one per group or the card statements so that each group has one set.
5 The level of task difficulty can be adjusted by restricting the number and/or complexity of the statements given to groups.
6 For Activity 3 *Controversial statements about science*, it is best to choose a selection of the statements and give the same statements to each group. But make sure that you provide **both positive and negative statements** to each group.

Please note that these statements are meant to be provocative to promote discussion and conflict. They are not intended to be correct, nor do they represent the views of the authors. There are many issues presented here – too many to comment upon. Pupils will come to this discussion, as you will yourself, with views which have either been inculcated or gained from prior knowledge. Each of the statements is intended to be a partial one-sided view about aspects of science. Some statements may be correct, others wrong. Sometimes all statements are correct but represent an incomplete one-sided viewpoint. The intention is to get groups to discuss the issues and come to a consensus as to what or how much they agree with, while contributing contrary statements to give a balanced view. It is hoped that this section will contribute to ideas and evidence about science whilst also addressing some of the greater moral issues in science which are current. Perhaps by considering a few of these ideas – both positive and negative – pupils may develop a better understanding and a more balanced idea of what science is and does.

Introduction

1 Start by eliciting from the class what they think science is. Alternatively, you can provide controversial examples of scientific activity and ask how many agree or disagree with the statement and why. Whatever you decide to use, keep it brief but pacey.
2 Introduce pupils to the task, either the questionnaire or one of the card activities.
3 For Activity 1 *Is this a science?* ask them to consider, in their groups, each item in

(T) This discussion could be initiated, for example, through thought showers or by direct questioning.

turn and decide whether it is a science or not. Emphasise that they should make a note of the criteria they are using to come to their decision. If the group cannot agree about an item they should note the reasons for disagreement.

4 For Activity 2 *Views about science* they have to decide whether the statements are valid and apply to science or not. Thus pupils could be asked to sort the statements into three piles: 'agree', 'disagree' or 'not sure'.

5 For Activity 3 *Controversial statements* give each group the same statements and ask them to comment on them. Is the statement true, partially true or false? Does the group agree or disagree with the general tone of each statement? Is there another side to the argument? Have some possible advantages/disadvantages or positive/negative statements been omitted?

6 Tell them that they will need to give their answers to the rest of the class in the plenary session and be able to explain **why** they had decided whether they agreed or disagreed with the statements or the views expressed.

7 If you feel that it would be helpful, you can take the whole class through one of the questions or cards to reinforce what is required.

Make judgements and decisions informed by evidence.

Develop criteria for judging the value of information.

As the activity focuses on argument and grey areas, some pupils may feel uncertain about the outcomes. Hard thinking does not automatically give you a clear correct answer. You may get a headache instead.

Group work

Pupils should work in groups of three to six to carry out the task. During this time you need to make class scans to check whether there are any major differences between groups that could be used in the plenary session. In Activity 3, especially, you will need to take notes during your class scans in order to plan a logical way through the plenary. In Activity 1 *Is this a science?* some groups had real difficulty in supporting their decisions with reasons. Where this happened it was worth helping them with one or two examples, building on the introduction, as well as stressing that the strength of science is in its explanations of phenomena and its predictive capacity. For example, in the case of astrology (once any confusion with astronomy had been clarified) pupils were asked if they had any experience of the forecasts coming true or not for them, friends and relations, and how they thought distant stars could influence minor events on earth. They were encouraged to 'weigh the evidence' and come to a conclusion.

Plenary

For Activity 1, the discussion should be managed using the observations which you noted during the group work. Feedback needs to be taken from each group to identify common areas of uncertainty or conflict. This focuses on:

- where there is disagreement and the reasons for the disagreement
- the general criteria which pupils use to identify a science.

Issues that arose from the questionnaire included the boundary between science and technology; whether scientific theories have to be open to testing; and how science theories are different from other theories.

In Activity 2 *Views about science* it is useful to aim to build up a bank of statements that everyone agrees are applicable to science and another of those which are not. You may have to have a middle group which are partially true or incomplete! In some lessons, further suggestions were made about other aspects that could be added to the lists. This built up a better understanding of which aspects are relevant to science – and, conversely, which are not.

Make deductions.

Activity 3 *Controversial statements* identified many misconceptions that pupils held. It may be difficult to lead this session since you may be led by your own beliefs. It is important to allow all pupils to have their say and to identify counter-arguments where possible. This is easier if you have identified these during class scans. The more you practise this session the more accomplished you will become at handling some of the arguments and counter-arguments and the more valuable it will become. It is important to emphasise that where theories are involved, there is no 'right' or 'wrong' answer. However, the use of evidence to support or refute a theory is an important point to bring out.

Evaluate information.

Generally where pupils had been used to having group discussions, they engaged well with the Activity and were able to make decisions and support these with clear argument.

Thinking Skills Through Science

Thus one group in a highly-attaining Year 9 class put forward the idea in Activity 2 *Views about science* that scientific theories were a mixture of statements 3 and 7. They were aware that 'school science' was rather like statement 7 but recognised that imagination played an important role in the work of great scientists. What came through clearly in this case was the importance of thinking through the evidence – and pupils clearly enjoyed and were stimulated by recognising that there may not be a single complete answer to the problem.

References

- *Children's Learning In Science Project*, Interactive Teaching in Science: Workshop for Training Courses, 1990
- *How Can We Be Sure?* Solomon ,J., (SISCON project), ASE,1983

Activity 1: Is this a science?   PUPIL SHEET

QUESTIONNAIRE

Discuss each statement on the list with your group and decide 'Is this a science?'
Record your group's opinion in the appropriate box.

	Agree	Not sure	Disagree
Acupuncture			
Aeroplane design			
Astrology			
Astronomy			
Biochemistry			
Car design			
Computing			
Cooking			
Creationism			
Economics			
Gardening			
Herbal medicine			
Meteorology			
Nuclear physics			
Physiotherapy			
Plumbing			
Space exploration			
Theory of evolution			
Theory of relativity			
Water divining			

You may wish to ask for definitions of some of the above terms or use
reference sources.

Activity 2: Views about science   PUPIL SHEET

1

Although some experimental results lead to different conclusions being made by different scientists, very careful observation sometimes shows that the conclusions are closer to each other than was first thought.

2

Science explains more as we learn more about things and gets us ever nearer the final truth about things.

3

Scientists produce theories out of thin air. They think them up out of their own imagination.

4

Different scientists explain the same evidence in different ways because they have different beliefs and values. For example, Muslims have different ideas of science to Buddhists, which are different to Christians, and so on. Aborigines have different viewpoints to Europeans, etc.

5

The more evidence there is, the more scientists are convinced that their theories are correct.

6

Science explains more and more as better instruments and techniques are developed.

Activity 2: Views about science (continued) PUPIL SHEET

7 Scientists collect data, sort and analyse it and then produce theories to explain the patterns in that data.

8 Scientists suggest explanations for things that happen and then search for evidence to prove it.

9 Science can explain virtually everything that happens in the universe.

10 The use of scientific ideas about energy, particles, cells, interdependence and forces help us explain many of the things that happen in the world.

11 To find answers to scientific problems, scientists take all the data and select those bits that best fit their ideas of what is happening.

Activity 3:
Controversial views about science

Science is about men things

Science is all about men in lab coats. Most scientists are men and women don't usually get a look in. They don't achieve anything anyway – it's all theory and maths. Einstein was a good example – an old man who was interested in space and produced these equations about space bending and black holes and things (aren't all holes black anyway?). Stephen Hawking is another example of a scientist. Science is about boring men stuff that isn't either interesting or important to our everyday lives.

Science makes life easier

Science helps us to cure disease. It is leading to longer life and helping us to live more comfortably. We have great new inventions like DVDs and PlayStation and digital cameras. We can eat lots of new things like ostrich burgers and bacon double cheeseburgers through new scientific techniques. We now have seedless grapes. When was the last time you found a bone in a piece of fish you were eating – all through new scientific techniques. Chickens are now much larger. Once upon a time we only had aspirin to cure a headache. Now look at all the pills you can buy over the counter to help do this. New medical techniques make it possible to transplant virtually every human organ – and so prolong life. Science is the best thing since sliced bread!

Science is dangerous

Science is dangerous and a waste of time. Scientists try out all these new ideas without knowing what might go wrong after a while. How do we know whether eating a genetically modified tomato might make our noses grow longer or even give us cancer? Anyway, what's wrong with all the tomatoes that we can now get, such as vine tomatoes and cherry tomatoes? Who needs science?

Science uses up the world's resources

Science uses up all of our resources. All of our oil is being used up in making petrol. All of our uranium is being used up in making nuclear bombs and running nuclear power stations. What a waste. We have horses and bicycles to travel – and we have our own legs. Why do we need cars? We hear of terrorists developing nuclear weapons of mass destruction. Nowadays virtually every country is using more and more uranium. Nuclear power stations use more and more of our resources – we could be using renewable energy resources like wind and wave power - and solar power like they use in Greek islands (on holiday, don't you notice that virtually all the water is heated by the sun?). Soon we will have no raw materials left. It is the scientists' fault.

Activity 3:
Controversial views about science

PUPIL SHEET

Science pollutes our world

Science is about theories and models. It doesn't work in practice, or at best it only partially works. There are always side effects. These side effects cause pollution. So nuclear power stations produce nuclear waste that we can't get rid of for thousands of years. Using certain refrigerants in our fridges causes the ozone layer to get thinner and increases our risk of skin cancer. Using petrol and diesel in our cars produces bad air for us to breathe. Burning fuels in cars and industry produces acid rain which kills our rain forests. It also produces global warming which is melting the ice caps and raising the level of the seas. All the industrial effluent pollutes rivers and seas and kills fish. Everything science does pollutes the world more.

Science and religion

Science is based on evidence and fair testing. This is why it is interesting and worthwhile. All of the things that science suggests are done by the 'scientific method'. This means that it is tested and tested again and so it must be right. You can trust science. It moves us forward to new things. It's not like religion which is based on things that might have happened in the past. Religion comes from stories that men wrote about many years ago – and some might have got twisted in translation and so on, so you can't prove that the stories are correct. Religion doesn't invent new things. Science is about the future – religion is about the past. You can prove what happened in science – you can't with religion.

Scientists invent great new technologies

Science is about inventors. Just think of the great new inventions that have helped us. Ever since early peoples produced fire, the wheel, and extracted copper and made bronze, science has been the driving force that moves the human race forward.
We have invented things like engines to make cars go, and fertilisers to help us grow more and better crops. We have built great bridges to span rivers, and machines to fly through the air. We have made computers that can process information very quickly. Medical advances have helped us cure disease and stop plagues like the 'Black Death'. We have found new and better ways of making fast food like Chicken Madras and KFC. Science has improved our civilisation like nothing else.

Science is bad news!

Scientists keep interfering with nature. Left alone, we would have clean air and unpolluted beaches, rivers and cities. Our food would again taste of something other than chemicals. There wouldn't be drugs like heroin and crack to cause all the crime and worry. There wouldn't be guns and bombs and so there would be fewer wars, and fewer people would be killed. There wouldn't be a hole in the ozone layer and we wouldn't have global warming. There wouldn't be all these old plastic bags blowing around causing environmental problems. All of these have come about because of science. Science is bad news!

Activity 3:
Controversial views about science

Science is what makes us human

Without science we would stagnate as a race. Science is what differentiates us from the animals. We have brains. Brains invent things. Once we have invented things we can't un-invent them. So even when one or two things aren't quite what we expected before they were developed, we still have to use them and learn to live with this. This is another thing that we need to thank science for. It helps us learn new things. This makes us more advanced and obviously better than the animals.

Science is a logical subject

Science is logical like maths. One thing leads to another and so you make progress. All these 'thinkers' of the past just jumped to conclusions and so you got silly ideas such as 'the Earth is flat' or 'I can change base metal into gold' or 'this woman is a witch because she put a curse on me'. There is still a lot of this illogical thought about in other subjects and life in general and it still leads to silly conclusions being made. Science is not like this. It builds on proof and logical thought processes.

Outline

The most common example of terminal velocity is probably a parachute and its use in skydiving. Pupils will be familiar with this, and will know that if something is dropped from a great height it speeds up. What they probably will not have considered is whether the objects which fall keep speeding up or not, and the reasons why. The idea of terminal velocity in a horizontal plane is probably much more familiar. All will have experienced the wind in their face when riding a bicycle, and the fact that it is easier to cycle downhill than uphill. In this case they will probably realise that in cycling up a hill they reach a maximum speed. They may not realise that this is also true of cycling down a hill, because the maximum possible speed is probably too fast to negotiate on the bike and brakes are applied. The investigation of these scenarios produces fruitful opportunities to develop thinking skills, because of the past experience of pupils and the cognitive conflict that this can cause.

In this exemplar, pupils are asked to look at these two different scenarios (a parachutist and a cyclist) and are presented with a velocity/time graph of what has happened in each case. They have to interpret each graph in terms of what the parachutist or cyclist has done to achieve the trace. As well as the graph, in each screen, they are given some visual clues as to what aspects (variables) may have changed during the run/descent.

The parachutist scenario (Activity 1) is used as a starter activity with the whole class to introduce the exemplar, and outline how to go about this sort of task. This starter activity may, in fact, take up to a whole lesson to complete and you may thus not get into the group work until the next lesson.

In the case of the cyclist scenario (Activity 2), pupils are given two initial runs where each of the variables is constant in turn, to aid interpretation of the other graphs. The activity can be split into two sessions if periods are short (less than a 50-60 minute lesson): the starter activity is done in the first and the main activity in the second.

Pupils' prior knowledge and skills

Although pupils will not meet terminal velocity by name until Key Stage 4, they will have met the concept as early as Key Stage 2. They will, for example, have experienced the concept of terminal velocity when they had made spinners weighted with paper clips in Year 6. They will be aware of parachutes and their effects and the fact that gravity is a force which acts downwards. However, before embarking on this activity, ensure that pupils know about the effects of a force in terms of speeding up and slowing down a body. It is also important that they recognise that forces act in a specific direction and the effect on any body is caused by the resultant of these forces (although it need not be put in these words). For example, they will be familiar with the fact that if two people push them equally from opposite sides then they don't move. If one stops pushing, then they do move!! They need to be familiar with the unit of force, the newton (N). The starter activity addresses these issues.

Links

QCA Scheme of Work	Thinking skills	Key scientific idea
Unit 9K Speeding up Unit 9J Gravity and Space	Information processing Reasoning Evaluation	Forces

Lesson objectives

Thinking skills:

- comparing and contrasting
- sequencing
- analysing relationships
- drawing inferences
- making deductions
- evaluating information.

(T) The main thinking skills objectives can be further broken down. Choose the most relevant.

Science:

- describe trends or relationships in graphs
- use arrows to represent the direction and magnitude of forces
- know that pairs of arrows can show balanced or unbalanced forces
- know that a force produces a change in speed (acceleration) and that air resistance is a force that opposes motion
- know that a slope increases or decreases the effect of gravity on a moving object (a bicycle) and so adds to or subtracts from the force applied to the pedals, thus affecting its velocity
- know that in the absence of a resultant force, objects move at a steady speed, or remain stationary
- know that when the upward force of air resistance balances the downward force of weight in a parachute, the velocity remains constant
- know that the effects of air resistance can be reduced by streamlining (and increased by reducing this factor)
- know that air resistance increases with increasing speed
- know that the energy (and force) required to keep a moving object moving depends on air resistance.

(T) Choose the science objectives that are most relevant to the group. **It is unlikely that you will be able to assess more than two or three.** Remember that your main objectives are thinking skills.

Context

As mentioned above, pupils will have had some previous experience of terminal velocity at Key Stage 2. They will have noted the differences in the time taken for the spinner to fall when different numbers of paper clips were attached. They will also have discussed the fact that parachutes slow down a falling skydiver. Working through this exemplar with Year 9 classes, however, addresses the more difficult science concept when treated in terms of the variation in forces acting on moving objects (it is a Year 9 unit in the QCA Scheme of Work). Also, the type of activity was new to most pupils. Although they had interpreted graphs before, they had usually done this to come up with a trend, such as the way in which liquids cool or how height varies with age. They had never used graphs to interpret what might have happened to produce this particular trace or line. For this reason, the parachutist scenario (Activity 1) was usually worked through as a whole class starter exercise to introduce the types of things that they might consider in such an exercise. Once they understood the principles, pupils were able to work together to agree on what might have happened in the other scenario (Activity 2). The teacher information sheets (pages 148 - 150) give some graph readings and further information for the cyclist scenario. You should read these before starting the activity.

A starter activity can often help pupils to prepare for the learning in the lesson.

Preparation

1 Photocopy the scenario sheets. Because interpreting the graphs is challenging, pupils need to see them closely to follow what is happening. It may be useful therefore to provide a copy for each pair of students. You may prefer to use larger A4 or even A3 sheets of each scenario and provide one per group. This will encourage interaction.

2 Make decisions about the ability of pupils in each group. The level of discussion will vary with the ability of the group. You may find that dividing the pupils into ability groups rather than mixed ability groups enables them to address the activity at their own level.

Introduction

Whole class starter activity

1 Discuss the fact that forces are measured in newtons and that forces make things speed up or slow down (as well as change direction and cause compression of objects, etc). There needs to be a discussion of the propelling and retarding forces, and that it is the resultant force which causes the change in velocity.

2 Pupils need to recognise that gravity is a force that acts downwards. At this point it is useful to work through the parachutist scenario (Activity 1). Make an overhead transparency and display the parachutist scenario on the screen. Highlight the various items of information which are given on the picture/graph:

- the different types of descent: (a) no parachute – free fall; (b) no parachute – sky diving; (c) parachute
- different sizes of parachute
- the fact that the picture (graph) represents what was happening to the trace at the moment the picture was recorded, ie the last point/bit of the line on the graph represents the situation as shown in the picture.
- the start velocity
- the changes in velocity over time as shown by the trace.

3 The best way forward is to ask what happened first. Most pupils understand that the parachutist starts off at rest and then quickly gets faster. In our classes, some brighter children wondered how the parachutist could start at rest: *'He must have been in a plane, which would be travelling quite fast – unless he jumped from the Eiffel Tower!'* This led to discussion of the fact that velocity is directional. The graph describes the vertical velocity of the parachutist, and most pupils were able to grasp this. This led to a discussion of acceleration (rate of change of velocity) with some groups. Other questions led into *'What was the fastest velocity that the parachutist ended up travelling?'* The next question usually caused some discussion: *'What happened next?'* All could usually see that the parachutist started to slow down, but there was some doubt as to what he/she had done to initiate this.

4 At this point it is useful to introduce the other two parachute scenarios, one at a time (you may need to place them side by side or have smaller transparencies to allow you to do this). You can probably see the way in which the discussion usually develops. The fastest velocity reached is noted as being different in scenario 3. The final velocity is different in all three. Usually, lots of interaction takes place as pupils discuss why there is suddenly a large drop in velocity (when the parachute opens).

5 In the end, most pupils, irrespective of their ability were able to see the factors involved and the effect that they had on the trace, and most developed through the discussion a better understanding of this (metacognition). If you have short lessons, this may be as far as you get in the first lesson.

Introduction to the group work

1 Pupils are introduced to the cyclist scenario (Activity 2). As in the starter activity, the layout of each screen needs to be described, so that pupils know what information is conveyed by each part.

2 The pupils' task in this activity is to analyse the information provided by the graph and decide what has happened over the period of the trace. It is important that pupils attempt the 'no slope' and 'constant pedal force' first, to come to terms with the variables and their effects (see Pupil Sheet, page 151).

Group work

Pupils worked in groups of three or four. Each group should agree on the sequence of actions that produced the trace and note this down, so that they can contribute better to the plenary. During this time you need to circulate among the groups, noting outcomes. If the groups are arranged by ability, you need to plan the order of input to the final plenary so that all groups have the opportunity to contribute, and to move their thinking forward too as the discussion extends beyond their current development. You can also use any major differences between groups to good effect during the plenary session.

The parachute scenario is easier than that of the bicycle. Once out of the plane, the parachutist must continue to travel DOWN and dares not close the parachute after opening it!

(T) Sequencing skills.

(T) In the end, by working through this example, pupils gained a better understanding of how to interpret graphs and to how to gain clues from all the information given. This stood them in good stead when they attempted the second activity which moved their thinking even further forward.

(T) Analysing relationships.

(T) Sequencing skills.

(T) Making deductions.

(T) Evaluating information.

Thinking Skills Through Science

Plenary

Manage the discussion using your observations during the group work. Less able pupils tended to take fewer variables into consideration during the group discussions. For example, they only considered a change in slope, or only considered a change in pedal force. With the recumbent example, many less able pupils did not note the difference of the effect of drag compared to the racer example. Certainly with more able pupils it is worth persevering with this so that the effect of drag is conceptualised. This is an extension to the size of parachute scenario in Activity 1 and a higher order thinking skill, since the force causing the effect is not controlled by the pupil, is not visible in terms of input and varies with shape and speed. This aspect did not seem to hamper the plenary discussion, providing the order of group input to the plenary was well planned. It is important therefore to take feedback from the different groups in the pre-planned order. The whole class should aim to come to a decision on which is the most 'popular' sequence of events? Why? Are there alternatives? What reasons do pupils give and what arguments are put forward to justify these? Further issues which might arise are discussed in the Teacher Information Sheets.

Follow-up

There are many aspects of this work which could be developed by further discussion, such as 'What if…?', 'How could we…?' and 'Is it possible to…?'. Other scenarios from different sections of work, using graphs from various sources, could be used.

More information on each scenario for teachers is shown in the notes on the Teacher Sheets.

(T) Compare and contrast.

(T) Drawing inferences.

(T) Evaluating information.

(T) Some pupils will remember relationships through the graphical representation.

Activity 2

Racer bicycle. No slope.

TEACHER INFORMATION

Actual sample. Changes in force applied to pedals.	
Force(N)	Velocity(m/s)
Start	0
250	9
350	12
450	16
150	5
50	2

Full force table. No slope.	
Force(N)	Velocity (m/s)
50	2
100	4
150	5
200	7
250	9
300	11
350	12
400	14
450	16
500	18

Activity 2

TEACHER INFORMATION

Racer bicycle. Constant force.

Actual sample. Changes in slope (force constant at 250N)	
Slope(°)	Velocity (m/s)
Start	0
0	9
-30	21
-15	15
0	9
15	3
30	0

Full constant force (250N) table	
Slope(°)	Velocity (m/s)
45	0
30	0
15	3
0	9
-15	15
-30	21
-45	27

Teacher notes.

Pupils should consider these two scenarios first before they move on to the other two bicycle scenarios. This gives an understanding that both variables affect velocity. The position of the force and slope gauges shows the setting of the gauges after the final change. This refers to the velocity trace at the right hand side of the graph (velocity shown on the velocity gauge also). These should give a hint to pupils to help to interpret the graph. Should further information be needed, pupils can be told that the start position of both gauges in both graphs was at 250N and no slope, although they should be able to work this out from a combination of the two graphs.

Activity 2   TEACHER INFORMATION

Racer bicycle. What might have happened?

Force (N)	Slope(°)	Velocity(m/s)
Start	0	0
250	0	9
350	0	12
450	0	16
450	30	4
450	0	16
450	-30	28
350	-30	25
250	-30	21
250	0	9

Teacher notes

Here, both the force and the slope change. Points to be addressed include the difference in effect of the two variables. It may be possible to have the same effect from different sets of values of the two variables. For example a force of 500N on an uphill slope of 15° and a force of 300N with no slope both give a resultant speed of 11m/s. It is not these absolute values that are important, but the fact that both variables have an effect on the velocity. Pupils should consider the fact that there is this quantitative interdependence. This hopefully will lead to some cognitive conflict and a fruitful plenary counter argument session, raising metacognition of the principles.

Recumbent bicycle. What might have happened?

Force (N)	Slope(°)	Velocity(m/s)
Start	0	0
250	0	11
250	15	3
250	-15	19
250	-30	26

Teacher notes

This scenario shows a trace of a ride on a recumbent bicycle at constant force (250N). Only the slope changes here, but there is a difference from the sample constant force trace shown by the racer. The resistance is less and the velocity attained by the same pedal force is greater. Pupils need to be able to come to this conclusion, so that the effect of drag is conceptualised. It may well come out in the plenary session from some groups but not others and needs to be addressed to aid construction processes.

Activity 2

PUPIL SHEET

No slope

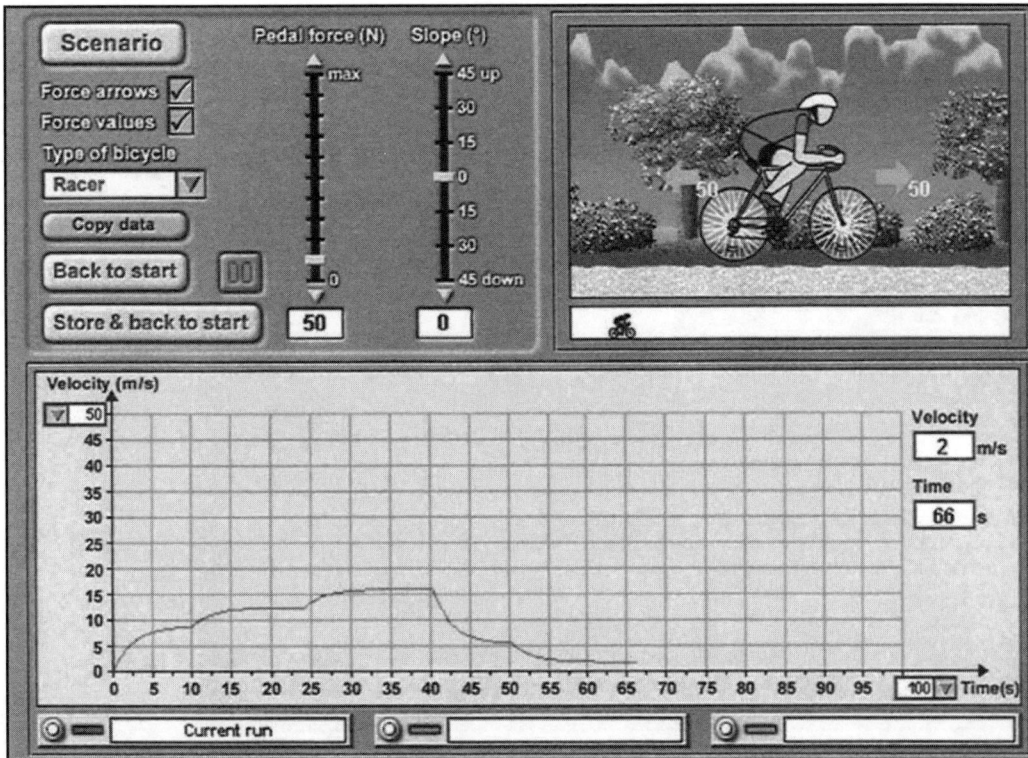

Constant pedal force

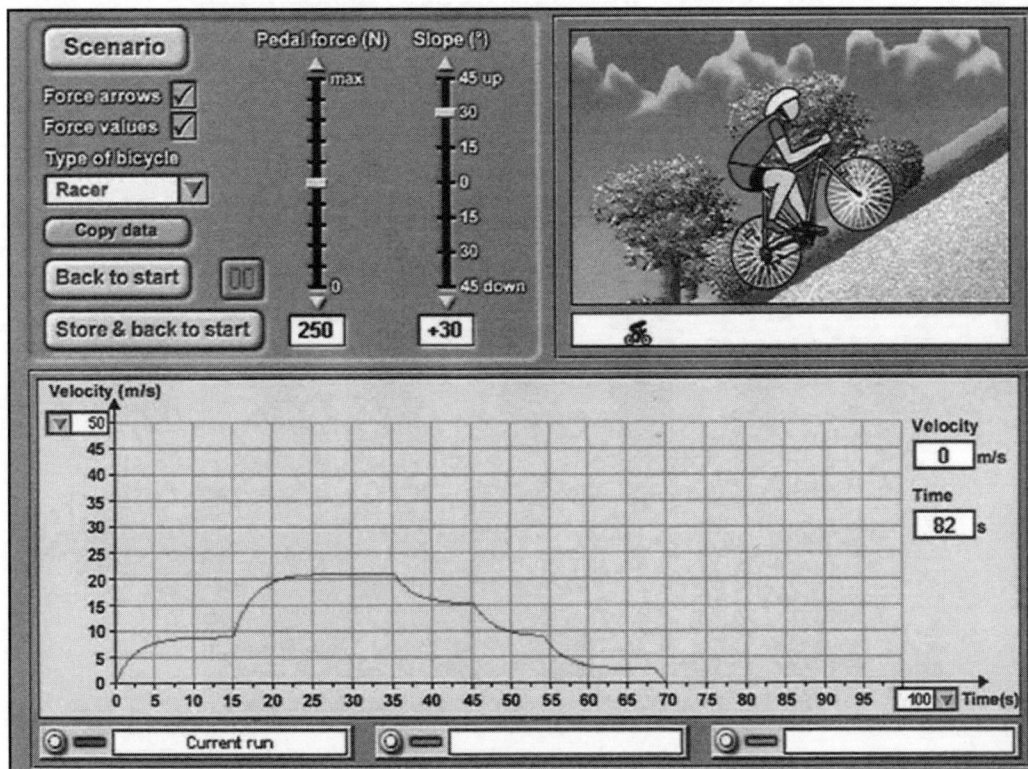

For ease of use, you can photocopy and enlarge the graphs printed in the text, or use the pdf file on the CDRom to print at a larger size.

Screens are reproduced from the teaching tool Terminal Velocity by kind permission of New Media Press, publishers of Multimedia Science School, a compendium of teaching tools for use in schools with students aged 12 to 16. Tel 01491 413999 Web site: http://www.new-media.co.uk

Activity 2

PUPIL SHEET

What might have happened 1?

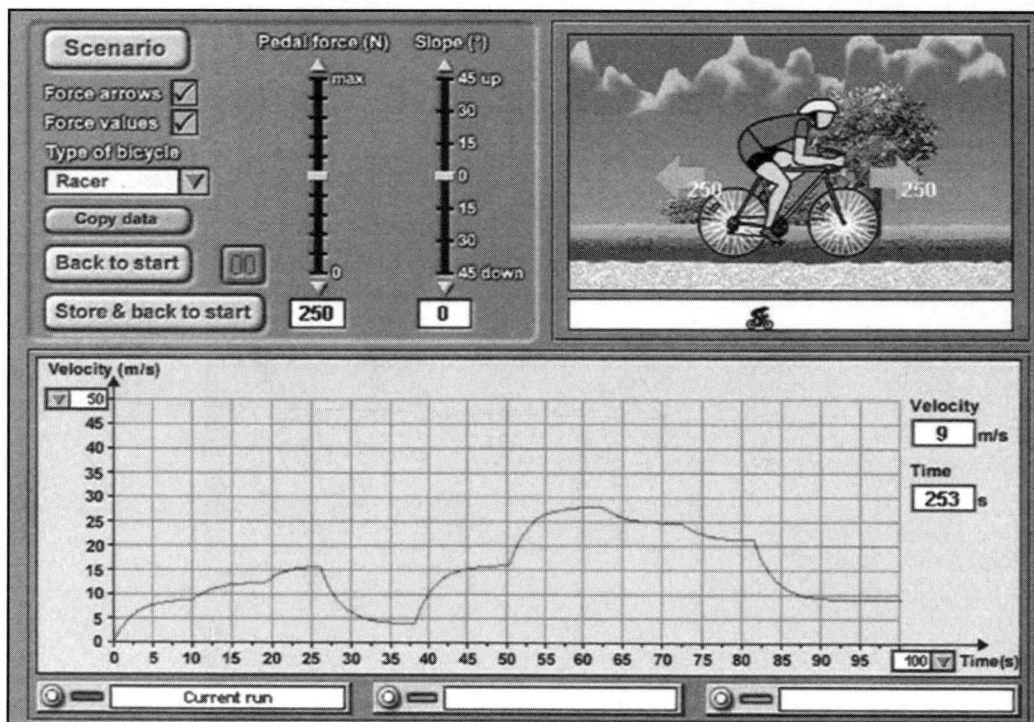

What might have happened 2?

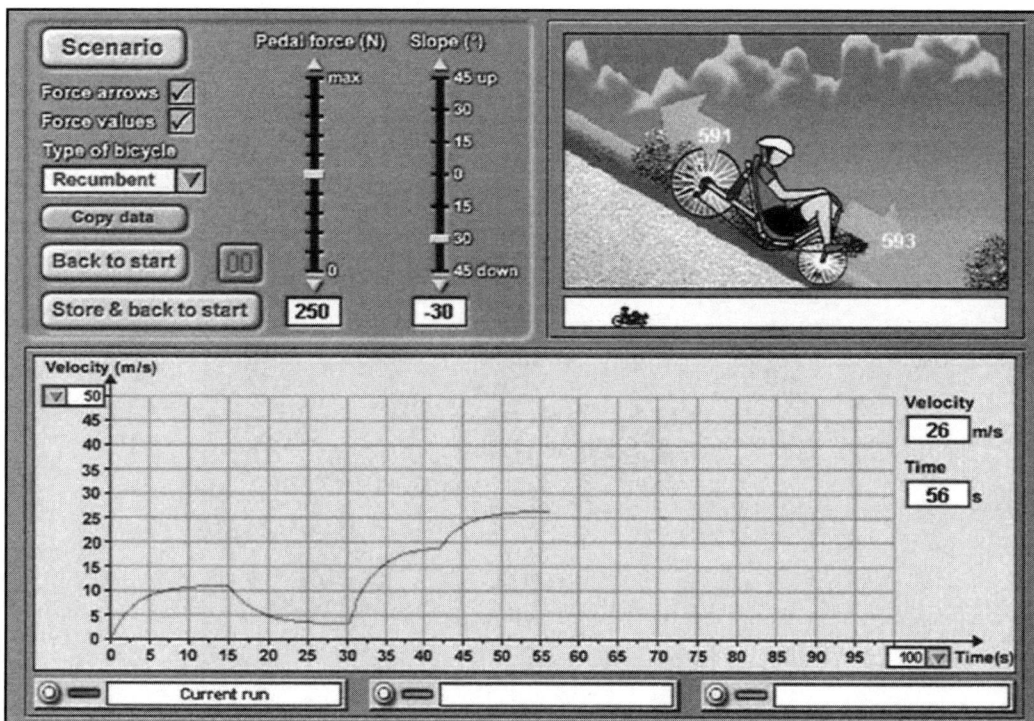

This bottom scenario is carried out at constant force (250N)

For ease of use, you can photocopy and enlarge the graphs printed in the text, or use the pdf file on the CDRom to print at a larger size.

Screens are reproduced from the teaching tool Terminal Velocity by kind permission of New Media Press, publishers of Multimedia Science School, a compendium of teaching tools for use in schools with students aged 12 to 16. Tel 01491 413999 Web site: http://www.new-media.co.uk

Thinking Skills Through Science

Activity 2

Parachute 1

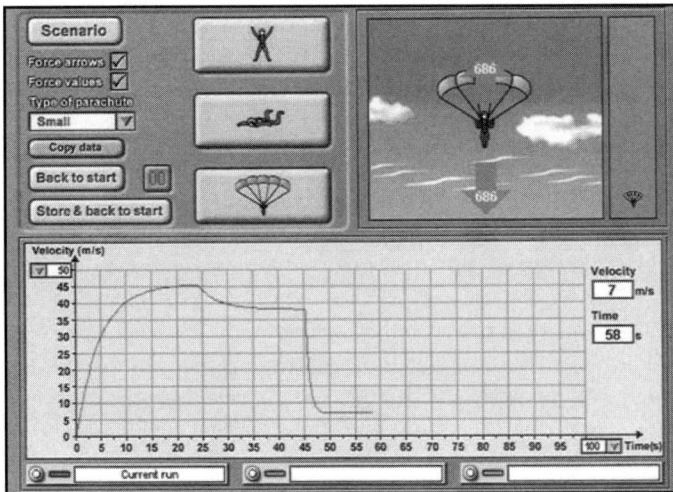

Parachute 2

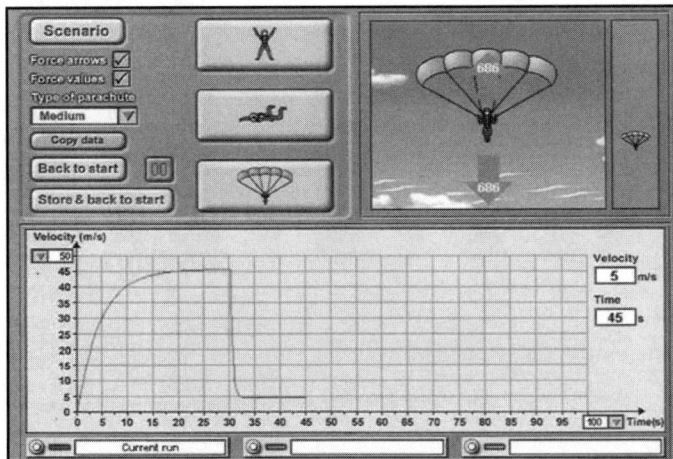

Parachute 3

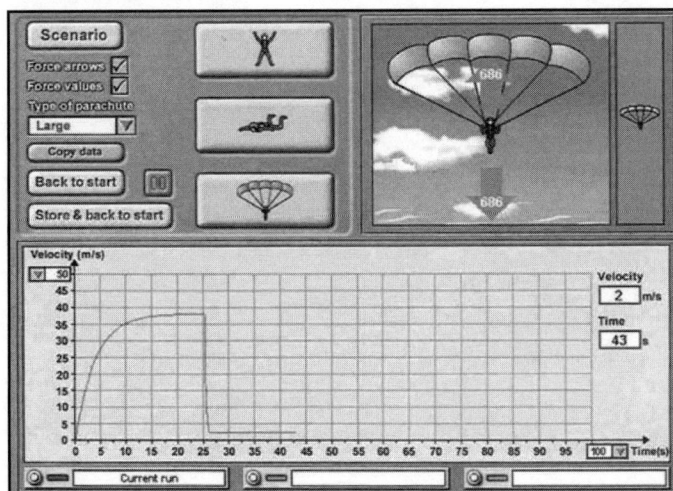

For ease of use, you can photocopy and enlarge the graphs printed in the text, or use the pdf file on the CDRom to print at a larger size.

Screens are reproduced from the teaching tool Terminal Velocity by kind permission of New Media Press, publishers of Multimedia Science School, a compendium of teaching tools for use in schools with students aged 12 to 16. Tel 01491 413999 Web site: http://www.new-media.co.uk

Outline

Stomach acidity is the topic of discussion in the best – and worst – of circles! Everyone has their favourite antacid tablet to counteract stomach acidity – and many people would swear that their tablet is the only one that works for them. Pupils too will have encountered these arguments, from granny swearing by her 'bicarb' to big sister not wanting to use these 'gritty pills that taste horrible'. So what is it that decides what a good antacid tablet is and does? Which is best? What does 'best' mean?

This exemplar asks pupils to decide which of a selection of antacid tablets is best to cure stomach acidity in the event of indigestion. They consider various properties of the tablets, including the 'active' ingredient, taste additives, 'chewability', price, number in a packet, etc. In order to explain the actual practical process for pupils, you may want to carry out a starter activity if pupils have not done this as part of previous work. You will then provide the available secondary data for pupils to discuss and come to a decision about which tablet is best for the job of curing acid indigestion, as well as their reasons for choosing this tablet. The relative importance of the various factors in making the choice needs to be understood.

Pupils' prior knowledge and skills

At the start, pupils have to come to some further understanding of the meaning of the word 'best'. At Key Stage 2 they will have become aware of fair testing and also the idea of 'best'. For example, they may have looked at investigations like 'What is the best trainer?' 'Which is the best paper towel?' or 'What material is the best for keeping us warm?' In this exemplar these ideas are reinforced and developed. Acids and alkalis are new ideas at Key Stage 3 and they will need to understand the basics of what these are, and how to test for them, in order to better understand the problem. In the past, these ideas have first been addressed when pupils have been doing chromatography in Year 7 for which they produce red cabbage extract or beetroot extract as part of developing manipulative skills with mortars and pestles. This extract has sometimes then been used as an indicator to introduce acids and alkalis. Although this activity can be developed at different levels during and after Key Stage 3, this basic understanding is necessary in order that pupils can come to grips with the factors involved.

Links

QCA Scheme of Work	Thinking skills	Key scientific idea
Unit 7F Simple Chemical Reactions	Evaluation	Particles

Lesson objectives

Thinking skills:

- recognise that 'best' can have different meanings for different people
- recognise that different factors have to be taken into account when evaluating the term 'best'
- recognise the need to make the test 'fair'
- develop criteria for judging the value of the result
- evaluate available information and increase confidence in judgements.

Science:

- recognise that carbonates can react with acids to usually produce neutral solutions (ie, remove acidity)
- understand that the body produces acid as part of the process of digestion and that sometimes this leads to over-acidity in our stomach which causes the pain known as acid indigestion.

(T) Real data can be used but experience has shown that this detracts from the thinking and tends to concentrate pupils' minds on the details of the practical instead of the thinking involved.

Science process is being unpacked at a fundamental level by really fretting away at what a simple word like 'best' means. It is usually used very subjectively.

(T) Although the basic thinking skill is evaluation, this can be further broken down.

Choose two or three objectives including at least one thinking skills objective.

Context

This has been carried out with a variety of classes, including a Year 7 class and, at the upper end, a Year 10 class. The degree of difficulty can be varied by altering the number of samples, the type of sample included, the way the information is presented and the inclusion of distractors within the information provided to the pupils (minty, chewy, etc) – if indeed you believe that these are distractors! (you may feel that being chewy is an important factor and so may the pupils). If the degree of difficulty is carefully judged then the exercise produces a fair amount of cognitive conflict. Pupils at all levels seemed to enjoy the exercise when this was the case.

Preparation

1 Identify the level of prior attainment of pupils in order to select the degree of difficulty appropriate to the class you are working with. You may feel that knowledge of acid/base reactions will be needed. This can be assessed prior to doing the activity by a quick question and answer session about the properties of acids and alkalis, methods of identifying them and removing acidity. But you may already possess this information, gleaned from work done during chromatography (see prior knowledge). If understanding is weak, you may wish to cover some preliminary basic ideas about acids and alkalis prior to starting the activity.

2 You may wish to select the amount of information given to pupils based on their prior ability. This may involve reducing the number of samples and/or the variety of information supplied.

3 You may also wish to change the quantities to make the calculations simpler for some groups and ensure that the mathematics does not get in the way of the thinking.

4 Photocopy the information sheets for the pupils.

> Information about sample antacid tablets that are currently available is given in the information sheet. These are based on real tablets available nationally.

Introduction

1 For the plenary to work well, all pupils need to have had the same experience, ie they need to have used the same data.

2 You may wish to begin with the following starter as a demonstration practical to show pupils the issues, techniques and the real practical scenario. In all the lessons that were tried, this proved to be a useful introduction so that pupils could better visualise the effects of their discussions in the real practical situation.

3 Pupils may have carried out the process before and a reminder may be all that is necessary.

4 Give the information sheets to the pupils. Make changes if you feel that this is appropriate. Carefully instruct pupils as to what the task is: to answer the question 'Which antacid tablet is best?' Explain that they should discuss the question in groups and come to a group decision. Ensure that any questions about the task or the starter demonstration practical are asked before they begin the main activity.

Starter demonstration practical

- A tablet is either broken up or ground up into a fine powder with a mortar and pestle and placed in a glass flask. Note that this introductory practical cannot use a chewy tablet.
- Five drops of screened methyl orange or red cabbage extract is added to act as an indicator.
- Acid solution is added carefully to the bits or powder in the flask. A burette is best here – although with some classes you may wish to use a dropping pipette to keep it simple.
- After each addition (or while the acid is being added), the mixture is swirled in the flask to mix the contents and help the gas (carbon dioxide) to escape.
- This is continued till the indicator changes to a red colour and stays red after swirling.
- The volume of acid added is carefully recorded.

> (T) Recognising the need to keep the test 'fair'.

> Active ingredient is not a factor if the results of titration are being used to determine acidity. If quantities (mass) of tablet are being used instead (at a higher level) then which active ingredient it is becomes important.

Group work

Pupils worked in groups of 3 or 4 to identify issues that are important in assessing 'best'. They used the available secondary data to assess which was best and why. In a few cases, as suggested under *Context*, they felt that the grainy taste of some tablets was a reason for them not to be best. Ensure that they understand the need to weigh up the relevant importance of some factors over others. For example, in this case the question was asked '...*and is this the most important quality that the tablet should have? Are other factors as important or more important than taste, or less important?*' Some groups felt that price was most important and that you should buy the pack which is biggest and cheapest (and not consider whether it actually was effective in the task of curing acid indigestion) – a common fallacy with grown-ups too! Averaging of the experimental results was an issue with some groups.

You should walk round and listen in to the groups to identify issues. Making notes may help. In order to incorporate them logically into the plenary session, you need to know which factors each group has discussed when making their decisions about 'best'.

Plenary

Lead the discussion of the group decisions, and the reasons the groups give. Class scans made during group work will have identified which groups can illustrate different issues. You need to be careful in planning the order of the group inputs to the final plenary. For example, you may feel that it is not ideal to approach the plenary by assuming that pupils think that the antacid properties are the most important. Let this come out through the discussion. It is important that the factors such as 'ability to cure acidity' are balanced by discussion about cost and other factors such as the number of tablets in a box, or/and mass, 'chewability' and 'peppermint taste'. The relative importance of these factors must be brought out in the discussion.

The most popular choices need to be identified and reasons understood (metacognition). In the end, there is not a correct answer for 'best' as some of the factors involved are subjective in some cases and may be more important to some people than others. Guide the discussion to ensure that it covers the two important factors: that the tablet needs to cure acidity and, at the same time, should not be too expensive.

Follow-up

No doubt you can extend this beyond Key Stage 3 using more complex scientific data, and where the active ingredient is not calcium carbonate (eg, tablets containing magnesium hydroxide, magnesium carbonate or sodium hydrogen carbonate bicarbonate). Further extension can be made by obtaining further data from real practical work. This could include use of a wider range of antacids, the accuracy of measurements in real practical work and the introduction of pH measurements (perhaps using data logging equipment and computer software). Rate of reaction may be a factor to be considered at higher levels.

All of these increase the difficulty in terms of science, not in terms of basic thinking skills, although the increase in the number and difficulty of variables will increase the cognitive conflict. Pupils will need to take into account more factors, which will have a more complex influence on the final decision. This needs to be borne in mind.

Sidebar notes:

(T) Recognising that different factors have to be taken into account when evaluating 'best'. This is metacognition at work.

(T) Developing criteria for judging the value of the result.

(T) Evaluating available information, and increasing confidence in judgements.

(T) Recognising that 'best' can have different meanings for different people.

You may use the data provided in the Information Sheets to devise further/alternative information to be included for pupils at a higher level. For example, if you do this with a good Year 9 or Year 10 class you may choose to include masses of active ingredient rather than titration figures.

Information about antacid tablets

PUPIL SHEET

Tablet	Volume of acid added (cm³) Experiment 1	Volume of acid added (cm³) Experiment 2	Volume of acid added (cm³) Experiment 3
A	16.0	15.6	15.6
B	10.0	9.6	9.7
C	15.3	15.0	15.1
D	10.2	9.9	9.9

Tablet	Number of tablets in pack (1)	Cost of Pack (1)	Number of tablets in pack (2)	Cost of Pack (2)
A	24	£2.25	48	£3.30
B	48	£1.80	96	£2.80
C	24	£1.60	48	£2.50
D	36	£1.75	96	£3.10

Tablet	Active ingredient	Additional information
A	Calcium Carbonate	Chewable
B	Calcium Carbonate	Peppermint
C	Calcium Carbonate and Magnesium Carbonate	Peppermint
D	Calcium Carbonate	Chewable

Antacid tablets: analysis

TEACHER SHEET

Sample analysis of antacid tablets available: their active contents and approximate costs.
These may be altered or added to for the purposes of this exercise.

Tablets A Chewable

Cost per packet = £2.25 (24 tablets)   £3.30 (48 tablets)
Each tablet contains   Calcium Carbonate 800mg

Tablet B Peppermint

Cost per packet = £1.80 (48 tablets)   £2.80 (96 tablets)
Each tablet contains   Calcium Carbonate 500mg

Tablet C Peppermint

Cost per packet = £3.80 (96 tablets)   £2.50 (48 tablets)   £1.60 (24 tablets)
Each tablet contains   Calcium Carbonate 680mg
                       Magnesium Carbonate 80mg

Tablet D Chewable

Cost per packet = £1.75 (36 tablets)   £3.10 (96 tablets)
Each tablet contains   Calcium Carbonate 500mg

Tablet E

Cost per packet = £1.99 (80 tablets)
Each tablet contains   Calcium Carbonate 200mg
                       Magnesium Carbonate 60mg
                       Sodium Bicarbonate 60mg

Tablet F

Cost per packet = £2.88 (60 tablets)   £3.66 (100 tablets)
Each tablet contains   Calcium Carbonate 520mg
                       Magnesium Carbonate 70mg
                       Sodium Bicarbonate 65mg

Tablet G Mint flavour

Cost per packet = £1.45 (24 tablets)
Each tablet contains   Magnesium Hydroxide 300mg

Science processes and understanding argument can both be developed. It is a rich activity.

Outline

This exemplar will develop pupils' thinking skills by using a context that is stimulating and interesting. Pupils are asked to evaluate statements relating to the extinction of the dinosaurs. They rank order them according to the most likely explanation. They must give reasons for their answers.

Pupils' prior knowledge and skills

Pupils need no specific knowledge other than an understanding that dinosaurs were animals that lived on the Earth millions of years ago. They were very successful and then became extinct.

Links

Possible link to Sc1 – ideas and evidence.

QCA Scheme of Work	Thinking skills	Key scientific idea
*Unit 7c Environment and Feeding Relationships.	Creative thinking Hypothesising	Interdependence

*The content is not directly related to this unit, but can be used to enhance the topic and to stimulate discussion and reflection.

Lesson objectives

Thinking skills:

Choose one or two thinking skills objectives.

- hypothesising skills
- creative thinking and the willingness to look at alternative explanations
- develop powers of reasoned argument.

Science:

- develop ideas about adaptation of animals to their environment.

Context

In Key Stage 3 pupils begin to learn about predator/prey relationships and, although evolution is not in the National Curriculum at this level, many pupils are interested in dinosaurs from an early age. This lesson was carried out with a Year 7 mixed-ability class. They had completed the QCA Scheme of Work unit on the Environment quickly, and this exemplar was an additional lesson that allowed all the Year 7 classes to move onto the next unit together. Although it was only intended to last one lesson (50 minutes) the pupils enjoyed the activity so much they asked if they could make presentations of the group findings to the rest of the class. This took up part of the next lesson and meant that they were behind the other classes for the next unit!

It would have been possible to reduce the time of the activity by reducing the number of statements the pupils had to order.

Some of the statements have an element of truth in them. In some instances there might have been a contribution to the extinction of the dinosaurs, but in others there probably was no causal effect.

Good for developing speaking and listening.

Preparation

1　Pupils should work in groups of three. The selection of the groups needs some care to ensure that the really keen, well-informed pupils are in the same groups. Past experience shows that when they are distributed between groups in an activity such as this, they tend to dominate the others. In this activity it is important that pupils discuss their ideas and argue from as equal a baseline of knowledge as possible.

2　Each group should have a photocopy of the key question on a large sheet of paper: 'Why Did the Dinosaurs Die Out'?

Sticking the cards on a backing paper enables the final order of each group to be recorded.

3　Photocopy the statements, cut them up, and place one set of the alternatives in an envelope for each group.

4　A blank sheet of paper could be given to each group to encourage them to note down their arguments to use as a prompt for their feedback.

Introduction

1 Set the scene by asking how many pupils watched the programme *Walking with Dinosaurs*. By careful questioning, you will probably find that some believed it was film of real dinosaurs. Some pupils can still hold this belief and yet know that dinosaurs are extinct. You need to be careful though, that pupils who do think that the dinosaurs in the film were real are not held up to ridicule. If you have an excerpt from the programme (or a similar film showing animated dinosaurs) it can be a good visual stimulus for pupils. You could have the sequence running as pupils enter the room. It's a good way to get their attention.

2 Begin with a brief starter activity where pupils brainstorm the names of animals and plants they know have become extinct. All pupils knew about dinosaurs, and a few knew of other examples – most of which they had picked up from television programmes.

3 Outline the activity. Tell pupils that all of the ideas on the cards have been put forward at some time to explain why dinosaurs became extinct.

4 Pupils should arrange the statements/cards in order, ranking them from the most likely to the least likely in terms of their influence on the extinction of the dinosaurs. Any cards which the group cannot agree on should be put together and discussed at the end. Any they still cannot agree about should be kept separate. Tell the pupils that they need to justify their ranking with reasoned explanations.

5 Some groups recorded notes of their reasoning to help them in the feedback.

6 Ask them also to try to make a prediction about the relative effects on population size, for instance would this lead to total extinction, extinction of a local population or the odd death?

> Assessment during the starter can enable effective grouping to be made.

> It is possible to 'guide' the lesson by careful selection of the statement cards issued.

Group work

The organisation of the groups worked well. Putting all the pupils with a good general knowledge of evolution and extinction together meant that all pupils could contribute to the discussions in the different groups. Most of the pupils loved the activity and found some of the statements funny. They did, however, find it difficult to justify some of their reasons. During the class scan it was interesting to note that, although there was some similarity between groups, there were also some major differences. These differences were used in the plenary to encourage pupils to justify their reasoning.

> (T) The difficulty pupils had in justifying their reasons is a strong argument for doing this type of task – rather than not doing it.

Plenary

Many pupils may choose the card referring to the meteor impact as a major factor in the extinction. Many will use information here that they have gleaned from television, although only partially. This could lead to a discussion about the need to read the statement carefully and to think through any assumptions, for example, how could a meteor have hit all the dinosaurs at once?

> (T) Checking assumptions is one of the basics of developing good reasoning skills.

Most pupils put statements referring to the Bible as having no effect. In this particular school this presented no major difficulties, although in other contexts these statements might need very sensitive handling or even not be used at all. It did, though, provide an opportunity to refer to the beliefs of others and the need for tolerance.

> (T) To develop a willingness to look at alternative explanations.

It is important to have a good idea what the pupils were thinking when they grouped and ranked the statements. The notes which you make in the class scan are important to guide the plenary discussion. For instance, some pupils had heard about small mammals eating dinosaur eggs but during the group discussions it was apparent that different groups placed different levels of importance on this. Knowing which group holds which view enables the discussion to be managed productively.

Follow-up

Quite a few pupils may be keen to carry out research to confirm (or otherwise) their reasoning and, if necessary, to reconsider the order in which they have placed the cards.

Statements

They were reptiles and more advanced forms of life evolved to replace them.	They were cold blooded.
There was a catastrophic climate change that meant they couldn't survive.	The ferns they lived on contained a laxative. When these ferns died out the dinosaurs became constipated and died.
The fossils we find that are the basis of proof that dinosaurs existed are discarded moulds from creation. One of God's mistakes.	The shape of the continents changed and new animals and plants arrived that were better at competing for food etc.
They just weren't good enough at surviving.	A small sun came close to the Earth and the radiation killed them.
Dinosaurs still exist - but as birds.	Small mammals ate their eggs so they didn't reproduce quickly enough to replace the adults that died.

Statements

They were too big to move quickly enough to escape their enemies.	A meteor hit them.
Noah forgot to take a pair on the ark and they drowned in the flood.	They didn't die out - there are still populations of dinosaurs in inaccessible parts of the Earth.
They were so big that if something attacked them from behind the messages to their brains took too long for them to react in time.	New diseases killed them.
Human beings killed them.	A big volcano erupted and changed the climate so they couldn't survive.
The magnetic field of the Earth changed; they became confused and couldn't find food or a mate.	

References

Adey P., Shayer M. & Yates C. (1995)
Thinking Science, Student and Teachers' Materials for the CASE project.
Walton-on-Thames: Nelson

Askew et al (1997)
Effective Teachers of Numeracy.
London: Kings College

Gamble R., Savory C. & McNiven D. (2000)
Raising Achievement through Thinking Science, A CASE North Initiative in
Education in Science. No 188, 28. Hatfield: ASE

Key Stage 3 National Strategy: Framework for Teaching Science: Years 7, 8 and 9. (2002)
London: DfEE ref 0071/2001

Learning and Teaching: Strategy for Professional Development.
London: DfES

Leat D. *Thinking Through Geography* (2001).
Cambridge: Chris Kington Publishing

McGuinness C. (1999)
From Thinking Skills to Thinking Classrooms: a review and evaluation of approaches for developing pupils' thinking.
London: DfEE

Naylor, Keogh & Downing (2003)
in *Science Teacher Education.* No 35.
Hatfield: ASE

Peasley K. L., Rosaen C. L. & Roth K. J. (1993)
The role of oral and written discourse in constructing understanding in an elementary science class. Paper presented at the annual meeting of the American Educational Research Association. Atlanta GA

Science: *A Scheme of Work For Key Stage 3.* (2000)
London: QCA

Shayer M. (1999)
'Cognitive Acceleration through Science Education II: Its Effects and Scope'
in *International Journal for Science Education.* Vol 21, No 8, 883-902

Shayer M. (2000)
GCSE 1999: Added-value from schools adopting the CASE Intervention.
London: Kings College

The National Curriculum for England: Science. (1999)
London: DfEE/QCA

The National Numeracy and Literacy Strategies and the Key Stage 3 Strategy.
London: DfES

Thorndyke P. W & Stasz C. (1980)
'Individual Differences in Procedures for Knowledge Acquisition from Maps' in
Cognitive Psychology. Vol 12, 137-175

Vygotskii L.S. (1978)
Mind in Society: The development of higher psychological processes
in Cole M., John-Steiner V., Scribner S. & Soubermann E. (Eds and Trans).
Cambridge, MA: Harvard University Press

Thinking Skills Through Science

References in relation to particular exemplars

For Exemplar 1: Alternative Science Theories

New Scientist, particularly *'The Last Word'*

Pasteur L. (1989) 'Stars and Forces, The Search for Simple Substances' and 'The Big Squeeze' in Solomon J. *The Nature of Science series*. ASE

Solomon J. (1983) *Science in a Social Context*. ASE/Blackwell

BBC programme *Simple Minds*

Wranglen G. (1971) in *Collection of Czechoslovak Chemical Communications*. Vol.36, 625-637

For Exemplar 2: A Burning Candle

Goldsworthy A., Watson R. & Wood-Robinson V. (1999) AKSIS *Investigations – Getting to Grips with Graphs*. ASE

Goldsworthy A., Watson R. & Wood-Robinson V. (2000) AKSIS *Investigations – Developing Understanding*. ASE

From Phlogiston to Oxygen. ASE

Children's Learning in Science Project, Workshop No 3 (1990). HMSO

For Exemplar 3: The Carbon Cycle

Lamb & Sington *Earth Story*. BBC Books

For Exemplar 4: Climate Change

Climate Change – Scientific Certainties and Uncertainties (2000) National Environment Research Council

Lamb & Sington *Earth Story*. BBC Books

Byatt, Fothergill & Holmes (2001) *Blue Planet*. BBC Books

New Scientist

For Exemplar 8: Evaluation of an Experimental Account

Lavens C. *Why Elephants Have Big Ears: Nature's Engines and the Order of Life*. Gollancz

Goldsworthy A., Watson R. & Wood-Robinson V. (2000) AKSIS *Investigations – Developing Understanding*. ASE

For Exemplar 12: The Solar System

Goldsworthy A., King R. & Wood-Robinson V. (2000) AKSIS *Investigations – Getting to Grips with Graphs*. ASE

Flavell & Tebbutt (1995) *Spreadsheets in Science*. John Murray

McNab & Younger *The Planets*. BBC Books

Websites including *www.rogerfrost.com*

For Exemplar 15: What is Science?

Children's Learning In Science Project (1990) Interactive Teaching in Science: Workshop for Training Courses

Solomon J. (1983) *How Can We Be Sure?* ASE: SISCON Project

Thinking Skills Through Science